The Reagan Paradox

The Reagan Paradox

American Foreign Policy in the 1980s

Coral Bell

Rutgers University Press
New Brunswick, New Jersey

First published in the United States of America in cloth and paperback by Rutgers University Press, 1989

First published in the United Kingdom in cloth by Edward Elgar Publishing Limited, 1989

Library of Congress Cataloging-in-Publication Data

Bell, Coral
The Reagan paradox: American foreign policy in the 1980s / Coral Bell
p. cm.
Bibliography: p.
Includes index.
ISBN 0-8135-1473-8 (cloth) ISBN 0-8135-1474-6 (pbk)
1. United States – Foreign Relations – 1981-1989. 2. Republican Party (U.S. : 1854–) – History – 20th century. 3. Reagan, Ronald.
I. Title
E876.B45 1989 89-33722
327.73–dc20 CIP

Contents

Introduction: Republicans and Foreign Policy

Republicans tend to have had rather a 'bad press' in foreign policy, especially in Europe. One could see that tendency as late as the second election of Ronald Reagan, in the car bumper-stickers reading 'Reagan in '84 – war in '85', or as early as the downfall of Woodrow Wilson, in the aftermath of the First World War, with US failure to join the League of Nations. The view of Republicans as not only more isolationist or unilateralist than Democrats, but as more likely to get the United States – and the world – into war was considerably reinforced in the late 1940s when the routine party-political assaults of the Republicans in Congress on President Truman and the then Secretary of State Dean Acheson were given a repulsive edge of savagery through the demagogic style of Senator Joe McCarthy. And some other Republican senators then were widely taken to be baying for an attack upon China and probably the Soviet Union as well.

But any assumption that the Republicans have been, in operational policy (as against rhetoric), demonstrably more careless of the maintenance of peace is rather at odds with the historical record. For in each of the five wars in which the United States has been embroiled this century, Democratic policy-makers took the vital decisions: Woodrow Wilson for the First World War, Franklin Roosevelt for the Second World War, Harry Truman for the Cold War and the Korean War, John Kennedy and Lyndon Johnson for the Vietnam War. Moreover, Republicans have presided over the three longest periods of détente during the tension-ridden decades since 1945: Eisenhower over the first (1953–6), Nixon and Ford over the second (1969–75) and Reagan over the third (1984–8). For reasons of ideological tact and his own past rhetoric, Reagan did not, even at the end, refer to his second term as a period of détente, but by all the criteria of diplomatic history it was one though not acknowledged as such.

This book will explore some of these paradoxes as they developed in the Reagan years and in the first months of President Bush. It may well be objected that the true dichotomy of opinion on foreign policy in the United States is not between Democrats and Republicans but between liberal internationalists and conservative nationalists, and that both those strands of opinion are to be found in both parties, whether one is looking at the grassroots level or the level of foreign policy élites. That is true, admittedly; but the blend of the two strands of opinion is by no means the same in the two parties, especially at the élite level, though the 'mix' is not quite as different on the two sides as it is, for instance, between Conservative and Labour attitudes on foreign policy in Britain.

Even before President Reagan's years of office there were a good many paradoxes in the relation between the world and the Republican Party. But he increased that level of paradox to a very notable degree. The role of George Bush in the decision-making of the Reagan years and the legacies which will influence his control of American foreign policy are examined in the final chapter. I have argued that he will face more complex but in several ways more hopeful choices than any of his predecessors, Democratic as well as Republican, in recent decades.

The election of 1988 reinforced the pattern which seems to have emerged in the late twentieth century for the Presidency to become a fief of the Republicans (Democrats have held it for only twelve years in the past forty) and Congress a fief of the Democrats, who often hold both House and Senate. That adversary-pattern as between the two main arms of government obviously increases their propensity, enshrined in the Constitution, to battle for the control of foreign policy. Those accustomed to parliamentary systems like the British, in which no equivalent would be possible, are sometimes disconcerted or worried by this constitutional dichotomy, but the world has to live with it and take it into account in all assessments of the future of American decision-making, in the four or eight Bush years. Reassuringly, examination of the Reagan years suggests that the situation is not without advantages.

1. Words and Deeds

American foreign policy experience during the Reagan years was rich in paradox: paradoxical in the most simple literal sense of 'contrary to expectations'. Who could have expected that a President who came to power on a well-orchestrated campaign against détente, and in particular against rash arms-control dealings with the dangerous Russians, would contemplate (as Mr Reagan did at Reykjavik and after) weapons cuts whose prospect initially stunned his NATO commanders and his West European allies? Or that a President who chose the combating of international terrorism as his central moral crusade would be brought to his most severe embarrassment over a deal to extricate hostages from the hands of terrorists? Or that the ancient Ayatollah in Iran could have been allowed to cast his shadow over a second President? To take a more hopeful line, who would have forecast that a President allegedly wedded to a rigid right-wing ideology could avoid serious frictions with both the major Communist powers, to such a degree that there would be no true crisis with either during his time on watch? (True crises in international politics have to be defined as episodes of heightened probability of hostilities between the powers concerned, not merely periods in which they are exchanging insults at above the standard rate. By that criterion there was no true crisis with either Moscow or Beijing in the Reagan years.) Equally at odds with the apparent ideological bias of the Presidency was the fact that a period expected by many people (approvingly on the right or disapprovingly on the left) to provide an 'easy ride' for the US's authoritarian allies in the Third World and a relaxation of pressure on South Africa saw, in fact, many Third World dictatorships falling into disarray, sometimes with a shove or two from various hands in Washington (though not usually the President's), and also saw American and international pressure on South Africa increasing to a degree that helped force some concessions, like the decision to pull troops out of Namibia and make at least some cosmetic modifications in domestic policy.

I have called those facets of US foreign-policy experience since 1981 paradoxes, but I shall argue that beneath all the improbabilities there was a built-in logic. That logic is to be found by examining the relationship between words and deeds, the declaratory and the operational policies of the administration.

In everyday life, and even in domestic politics, a marked disparity between words and deeds will naturally attract the charge of hypocrisy. In a sense, that must be so in foreign policy as well, but the relationship has more complexities than can be conveyed in such a dismissal. Mr Molotov once said that words *are* deeds in international politics, and though not many of Mr Reagan's aides are likely to have sought counsel from that old Stalinist, the technique of making words stand in for deeds, images for substance, was certainly well-enough developed in the Reagan years to be classifiable as a foreign policy technique. Though in late 1986, in combination with other factors, it produced the embarrassing fiasco of 'Irancontragate', in earlier years it had shown some successes. An apologist might have called it a form of economy of force, and argued that on the historical evidence it avoided more dangers than it incurred. That argument became harder to sustain after the Iran imbroglio, which did undoubtedly reduce American diplomatic leverage, at least for the last two years of the Reagan period. It did not diminish the chance of further progress in arms control agreements with the Soviet Union, but allowed little scope for other foreign policy initiatives until there was a new occupant in the White House.

Well before the Iran imbroglio, by the beginning of President Reagan's second term, some of his original right-wing supporters seemed as much at a loss as his original left and liberal critics to provide convincing interpretations of his foreign policy. How ought one to construe the contrast between the readiness for the summit meetings with Gorbachev from 1985 with the 'evil empire' rhetoric a few years earlier? A case of oratorical false hair on the chest? A dove temporarily decking himself in hawk's feathers, but discarding them when they had served an electoral purpose? Was the case, alternatively, perhaps that of an innocent American ideologue being 'snowed' by crafty West Europeans, the Washington bureaucracy and the American foreign-policy establishment into a reluctant and unnecessary pragmatism? Or was Mr Reagan originally mistakenly identified with the company he initially kept, assumed to be a far-right 'true believer' in foreign policy merely because he had found the far right, in general, useful in his 1976 and 1980 bids for the Republican nomination, and for victory in the first election?

Contrariwise, with not too unreasonably generous a dose of charity, it was possible to make the case that the President's policy was essentially consistent, in the sense that his aspiration had always been 'negotiation from strength', and unlike the earlier exponents of that concept in American foreign policy, he did, in fact, manage a sufficient level of apparently rebuilt military, political or diplomatic strength during his first term to warrant moving logically on to the 'negotiation' side of that double-barrelled concept in his second term. That rather flattering interpretation was tenable during the first six years, and implied the possibility that President Reagan might pull off an aspiration that such earlier masters of the arena of international politics as Acheson and Dulles had been obliged to relinquish, and secure a success that the earnest, well-informed, well-meaning 'workaholic' President Carter had become nowhere near. For reasons to be examined presently, that chance appeared quite strong in 1985, but had vanished in all but one respect by the end of 1986.

Even his kindest friends did not attribute to President Reagan any profound knowledge of world affairs, or any deep understanding of the subtleties of diplomacy. Or even an undue devotion to mastering his 'briefing books': he was clearly from the first an intuitive or instinctive politician rather than an intellectual or a particularly hardworking one. It was always rather more plausible, therefore, to see him essentially as an amiable American image, an actor with, usually, the knack of putting conviction into whatever scripts fate or history (or his aides) thrust into his hands. Thus one could argue that the anxieties of the American people after the traumatic events of 1975–9 in effect dictated the script for his abrasive earlier style, whereas the more relaxed national mood of the mid-1980s permitted his emollient later style. Except when his luck deserted him for a while in late 1986, no one doubted the President's perfect understanding, by long training as well as intuition, of 'what will play in Peoria'. One might say his speech of March 1987, replying to the Tower Commission report, was a masterly display of that particular talent.

That interpretation would entail the assumption that the

American system as a whole was on 'autopilot' for much of the time. And the 'autopilot' in question would have to be identified as primarily the bureaucratic machinery. Until the Iran fiasco, it seemed possible to argue that the system actually worked better on that basis than with an active interventionist Chief Executive like Jimmy Carter constantly adjusting the helm. But Iran showed the necessity for genuine diplomatic understanding and control *somewhere* near the highest level. A President who may tend to nod off on his watch needs at least a reliable helmsman and navigator, and neither seemed to be on deck for a while.

But finally, the whole Reagan experience, and in a different way that of Jimmy Carter as well, seemed notably to illustrate Machiavelli's reflections on the relationship between *fortuna* and *virtu* in political leaders. For his first six years, and again after the recovery from the Iran imbroglio, President Reagan seemed to have enlisted the goddess of fortune as his personal guardian angel. And *virtu*, in the sense not so much of good intentions (though those were real enough) as of virtuosity, an acquired skill in performance (specifically of communication) accounted for a good deal of the rest of his successes. By contrast Jimmy Carter did less well on both counts.

Only a much longer period of historical retrospect will determine which, if any, of those interpretations can be made to stick. But they all seem worth exploring, and this study will explore them.

The logical point at which to start seems to be with the reasons why the President, after a time, became rather a disappointment to those who had originally seen him as the true standard-bearer of the right in American foreign policy. That had long been 'a role waiting for a hero' (as President Nasser once said of his own emergence in Egyptian politics) and by 1980 Ronald Reagan seemed to have been selected by the central casting bureau of history to fill it. By 1985, in contrast, the leading gurus of the right were expressing a serious disenchantment. The *New York Times* interviewed a group of them and reported anger, frustration, puzzlement and general disillusion.[1] Ascribing reasons for that turnabout involves looking at assorted foreign policy stances of the right as well as at Ronald Reagan's particular style and techniques in foreign policy and his place in the overall spectrum of American political feeling. There are as many shades of blue in that spectrum as there are shades of pink in the spectrum of European left-wing opinion, but this point was not much appreciated by Mr Reagan's European critics, who were not usually acquainted with the finer distinctions between American conservatives, neo-conservatives, new right, Moral Majority or Liberty Federation and plain Republicans. For reasons which will be further explored later, it was the neo-conservatives who were assumed by analysts in Western Europe and elsewhere to be the most influential in foreign policy matters among the diverse confederation of the right which was assumed to be likely to come into power with Ronald Reagan. That is, they created his initial foreign policy image outside America. Their achievement of that rather misleading success derived partly from the fact that, though the neo-conservatives are exceedingly few in numbers compared to other right-wing groups ('all chiefs and no Indians'), they are mostly highly articulate intellectuals, working as editors, journalists or academics. Many of them are professionally in the business of defining political issues and positions, and make comfortable livings by doing so as syndicated columnists and such. So their arguments tended to be more skilful and quotable than those of larger, less articulate, less interesting (to outsiders) groups of Reagan supporters. And that characteristic articulacy of the neo-conservatives meshed in with a very notable general change in the international system, a change relevant both to the evolution of President Reagan's diplomatic *persona* and to the central argument of this book.

The contemporary international system is much more dominated than any earlier model by the means of surveillance and communication. A great, incessant, unstoppable Niagara of communications now flows to every corner of the world, often at literally the speed of light, courtesy of the electronic wizardry of our day. The inputs to this global torrent – the individual drops of water that make up Niagara – are called 'signals'. It is from assorted incoming signals that every society creates its own images of other societies. But national inputs into the general world-flow of signals are quite unequal: some societies are much more abundant as sources than others. The dominant mainstream for most of the world undoubtedly flows from America: perhaps it supplies as much as all the other members of the society of states put together. The Soviet Union contributes only a rather thin trickle of signals: the West and East Europeans considerably more. The Third World provides a very erratic flow: when there is some great disaster a temporary cloudburst of signals suddenly arrives from the afflicted society, otherwise very little gets into global circulation. (Third World governments naturally resent the dichotomy between media 'overkill' in their bad times and massive lack of attention in normal times, but it is probably inherent in the popular definition of news.)

The central point for this analysis, however, is that each society's general image of every other society in the international system (and especially of its current policy-makers) is made up of a selection (often arbitrary and idiosyncratic) of the signals that are diffused in this manner. The policy-makers in each national capital do get a larger assortment of signals than their respective general publics, because they have other sources to supplement the media: reports from their diplomatic and intelligence communities, for instance, and face-to-face encounters with policy-makers from other societies. And those who are professionally in the business of 'reading the signals' from the outside world (diplomats and intelligence analysts) may have a very sophisticated basis of selection. Nevertheless, they all have to face the ambiguities of balancing 'declaratory' against 'operational' signals.

That distinction was not invented for Ronald Reagan's foreign policy, but if it had not already existed, it would have needed to be. It first came to the notice of the author in an article by Paul Nitze on the foreign policy of John Foster Dulles,[2] but it is applicable, in greater or lesser degree, to all governments and administrations everywhere.

Obviously, 'operational' signals derive from what a government *does*; 'declaratory' signals from what its members (or those who are assumed to speak for them) *say*. This dichotomy has no doubt always existed, but the vital difference between the present situation and the past (even as recent a past as John Foster Dulles) is that the communications revolution seems to have now greatly magnified the impact, particularly, of declaratory signals. A neat example of that, in Mr Reagan's time, was his rash little joke, when a microphone was being tested 'We begin bombing in five minutes'. The original American 'shot heard round the world' was an *operational* signal; that 'joke heard round the world' was a *declaratory* signal. (No doubt an inadvertent one on Mr Reagan's part, but to some of his auditors all the more significant for that reason.)

It has become a cliché to talk of the 'global village': nevertheless, the image of a village for the contemporary surveillance-and-communications-dominated society of states is inescapable. Concentration on personalities, not only for Mr Reagan and his political entourage but also on their Soviet 'opposite numbers' (including 'first ladies'): the unstoppable growth of 'instant comment' whose providers fill much of the traditional interpretative function of the gossips in the village pub; the impossibility of hiding or ignoring disaster, distress and dissent; and the difficulty of keeping secrets (though some of the national families in the global village are better at it still than others): all that reinforces the image. So does the feeling that the dominant feud between the two most powerful village clans may bring a (radioactive) plague on all our houses. Even economically, one could say the society of states is now a single global market, for capital as well as goods, in a way it never was in the past, with consequences well-illustrated by the impact, world-wide, of the great Wall Street crash of 1987.

To return to the distinction between operational and declaratory signals, though there is always, for any government, some disparity between them, these distances range from a smallish gap to a considerable chasm. One of John Foster Dulles's chief aides, Robert Murphy, once wrote that you had to take many of the things Dulles said 'with a whole warehouseful of salt'. On that matter, as on several others, the Eisenhower–Dulles period seems the true exemplar and predecessor of the Reagan period.

The resemblances will be more fully explored in the next chapter. Meantime, though the Iran débâcle over hostages and arms sales illustrated perfectly the problems that arise when declaratory and operational policies are too much at odds, that does not mean that declaratory signals should be dismissed as hypocrisy or hot air, nor is a gap or even a chasm necessarily always a matter for surprise or regret. The French have a saying, 'The soup is never eaten as hot as it is cooked'. Translating that for our purposes, one might say that in any society the hot soup of declaratory policy, as it emerges from the hands of the ideological cooks who prepare it, is necessarily cooled a bit by the breath of pragmatism before it is served up as policy. Or to change the metaphor, one could say that the two sets of signals have complementary functions, the declaratory ones setting up 'Thin Ice' signs where the dangers have to be emphasized, the operational signals indicating areas where movement may be possible.

What must also be noted is that the two groups of signals derive from different elements in the political cast of players, at least in the West. (Differences between the US and the Soviet Union on this matter will be examined in more detail presently.) Declaratory signals come not merely from Presidential rhetoric and from what I shall call the 'entourage' of each President (the speechwriters and other political appointees who come into office on his coat-tails, as against the permanent bureaucracy) but from the gurus: that is the journalists and academics and publicists who sponsor, interpret, diffuse and applaud the concepts that become attached to the candidate in the very long process that precedes his election. They also come from the society as a whole, at least in the pluralist West, especially in the US which constantly diffuses signals of the national *mood*, which must be taken into assessments (especially by outsiders) of the governmental *will*. By contrast, the operational signals – from things actually done – must derive from decisions taken by the President and his immediate policy-entourage, though minor ones may originate somewhere in the enormous bureaucratic machine that serves him.

One very important group of signals lies on the borderline between declaratory and operational policies, or may move from the first category to the second within a few years. The proposed Reagan defence budgets, for instance, could originally, in 1981–2, be classed as primarily declaratory signals: that is, statements of intent about the *future* balance of forces. From 1983–4, such changes as were effected would need to be classed as operational signals. (Similarly with the Strategic Defense Initiative (SDI), a point developed later.) In some circumstances even an actual military operation might be primarily a declaratory signal, if the 'target audience' was not so much the people in the area concerned but a larger outside group. The US intervention in Grenada, for instance, could be regarded as primarily a declaratory signal to a world audience outside that tiny island, an audience far more important than Grenada itself as an element in international politics. The strikes against Libya might be regarded as an operational signal to the decision-makers of that small society, but of equal importance as a declaratory signal about the possible risks of sponsoring terrorist operations to a wider audience, mostly Arab but including Iran.

If a farmer, observing a boy robbing his apple-orchard, merely 'cusses him out', that is a declaratory signal. If he takes after him with a stick, that is an operational signal. But if he shakes a stick at him, that is an ambivalent signal; the boy (and any other boys watching) will interpret it as declaratory or operational in accordance with the conviction put into the performance.

The declaratory signals which originated mostly with the entourage and gurus of the Reagan camp must be particularly borne in mind in understanding why the neo-conservative contribution to the initial image (as against the policies) of Ronald Reagan, was so decisive in the way he was regarded outside America. Though all the groups making up the right-wing confederation were, of course, anti-communist, and quite strongly reassertive of American values and interests, not all of them were primarily orientated to foreign policy. The fight against abortion, or against the 'busing' of schoolchildren, or for the restoration of prayer in schools, or the defence of the family against 'gay rights', may be for most of the right-wing rank and file matters of more passionate concern, day by day, than keeping up with the latest developments in Soviet–American relations. Thus the neo-conservatives came rapidly to be seen, especially by outsiders, as the foreign policy specialists of the Reagan confederation, as the 'Committee on the Present Danger'[3] came to be seen as its defence specialists.

And yet in some ways the neo-conservatives were always rather incongruous allies for a Republican contender for the Presidency. For one thing, a lot of them were (and some still are) Democrats, the movement having originated within that party. Quite a few had been associated with a one-time Democratic hopeful for the Presidency, Senator Henry Jackson. Richard Perle, undoubtedly the most adroit and influential among the Reagan neo-conservative policy-makers, had earlier been Henry Jackson's chief aide. Jeane Kirkpatrick, whose rhetoric as US Ambassador to the UN was a major factor in creating the Reagan image abroad, remained a Democrat until 1985. Norman Podhoretz who, as editor of *Commentary* and a lively, widely-syndicated journalist, has been perhaps the most articulate spokesman of the movement, still defines himself as a Democrat. Daniel Patrick Moynihan, Irving Kristol and Nathan Glazer as sociologists or philosophers of ideas seem to have more affinities with the Democratic than the Republican mainstream.

The name 'neo-conservative' is in any case rather a misnomer. As Norman Podhoretz observed in a very influential article,[4] 'there are grounds for wondering in what sense most members of this group are conservatives, "neo" or any other variety'. They might more accurately be described as radical-right American nationalists, though that would require adding something to distinguish them from other radical right-wing American nationalists. The phrase 'liberals who have been mugged by reality' contains an obvious element of self-flattery, but it also has substance, in that many of the group originally held left-liberal or radical or even Trotskyite views, and the moral intensity of their later right-wing radicalism seemed rather a mirror-image of an earlier intensity of left-wing radicalism. They might, in fact, be seen as 'revolutionaries of the right' rather than conservatives, in that they wanted to change things, reverse tendencies and developments they saw as disastrous, rather than maintain the status quo.

European ex-communists have often said that the final battle would be between the Marxists and the ex-Marxists: meaning that a disillusioned 'true believer' is the most dogged and bitter and also perhaps the best-informed of enemies, since he has lived inside the adversary camp. There was something of that feeling of 'knowing-the-enemy-better-than-you-do-because-I-have-lived-with-him' in what was to become the central foreign policy tension of the Reagan period, that between the neo-conservatives and the traditional conservatives, a conflict which will be looked at in more detail presently.

In passing, it is perhaps worth noting that neo-conservatives tended to seem rather odd bedfellows to many other elements of the Reagan right-wing confederation. They were intellectuals and élitists, whereas most of the big battalions of the right were populist, anti-élitist and sometimes rather anti-intellectual. The neo-conservatives tended to be of Jewish or Catholic background, and many of them seemed to have lapsed or graduated to secular humanism. A large part of the 'new right' was Protestant fundamentalist, suspicious of Catholics, sometimes anti-Semitic (though in other cases ardently pro-Israel), and even more averse to secular humanists than to adherents of either of those two religions. However, in foreign policy matters the New Right did not produce anything much save the 'Armageddon' theory[5] which some equally way-out left-wingers were at one stage endeavouring to attribute to the President. So the true intellectual battle, on foreign and defence policy, during the Reagan years may best be seen as between the neo-conservatives and the conservatives, and it is to their differences we must now turn.

On many foreign policy points they did, of course, see eye to eye. Both groups assign great importance to balance-of-power analysis as a guide to foreign policy decision-making, both asserted the fundamental point that Soviet power had increased, was increasing and must be contained or, if possible, diminished, since it offered an 'implacable challenge' (originally George Kennan's phrase,[6] but much quoted by Podhoretz) to the survival of Western values, institutions, power and interests. But the point on which neo-conservatives differed from traditional conservatives, and the source of their original usefulness to the Reagan camp in the first unsuccessful bid for the Republican nomination against Gerald Ford in 1976, was that they came to a far more pessimistic 'bottom line' than the conservatives in making the balance-of-power assessments which underlie the policy prescriptions of both.

Those assessments were crucial to judgement of the US–Soviet détente of 1969–75. Détente was and is essentially a conservative concept: its postwar exponents have included not only Nixon and Kissinger but such unimpeachably conservative nationalists as Churchill and de Gaulle; likewise all or most of the thoroughly conservative and traditionalist foreign-policy establishments of Western Europe. But in late 1975 Moscow's decision-makers had embarked (in Angola) on the course of diplomatic opportunity-snatching in the Third World which brought the word into at least temporary disrepute, though much more so in the US than in Europe. For anyone needing in 1976 a club to attack the foreign policies of the Nixon–Ford–Kissinger era, a well-elaborated case against détente therefore came in very handy. And the most extensive repertoire of anti-détente articles to be found in any publication was and is in *Commentary*, published by the American Jewish Committee, the house-magazine of neo-conservatism. Thus the intellectuals associated with *Commentary* became useful tactical allies of the Reagan camp, although the US Jewish community in general had traditionally been associated with liberal-democratic causes, and in 1984 it swung against Mr Reagan, possibly fearing his connection with Protestant fundamentalism, which has often been anti-Semitic. (In 1988 it was with Dukakis).

The differences over détente, though exceedingly important politically and diplomatically, may also be seen as symbols of larger intellectual differences. Neo-conservatives see (or at any rate, depict) the world of international politics in black and white: a Manichean struggle between good and evil. The traditionalist conservative takes a philosophically Hobbesian view of international politics, seeing the 'war of all against all' as the always-contingent outcome of a situation in which there is no common sovereign, nor likely ever to be one. The techniques of *realpolitik* are seen to offer a mode of survival in that situation, and more optimistically a long-term chance of mitigating conflicts or of inducing some semblance of order. It is not a doctrine which requires heroes or villains, or which attributes special wickedness or special virtue to any of the polities in the system. It is therefore a view which has the intellectual merit of being applicable as a theory to all systems of international politics, as relevant to the relation between Athens and Sparta in the fourth century BC as to that between Washington and Moscow today. Neo-conservatism does not have that kind of timelessness and universality or detachment: it is a doctrine specifically about the relation between Moscow and Washington in the late twentieth century. It does have heroes (Washington and Israel) and villains (Moscow, Libya, Iran, Nicaragua, Vietnam). That was precisely why it had a wider popular appeal, at least within the US, than traditional conservatism.

Few things are more likely to be well-regarded and well-received than telling people what they want to hear. Americans, after the dispiriting years of Vietnam, the trauma of Watergate, the humiliating months of the hostage crisis, wanted to hear that the American cause was righteous, its political and social values uniquely meritorious, and that its allegedly sapped military strength could and would be rapidly restored. As Reagan put it, the country would 'walk tall' again. Neo-conservative doctrine put an intellectual gloss on those artful Reagan simplicities, though Mr Reagan's own foreign-policy stance by his final years of office had come to look more like a sort of right-wing Utopianism of a simplistic kind rather than a coherent neo-conservatism or traditional conservatism.

Conservatives regard the Soviet Union as a dangerous but cautious adversary power, espousing political values that a conservative must find repugnant, as well as an economic system of demonstrated inefficiency. And they therefore have no doubt that the growth of Soviet power must assiduously be balanced, and the growth of its influence contained or offset by all diplomatic means possible. But they would hold that this is a situation not unlike many that have existed between 'adversary pairs' in the past, and that diplomatic history offers techniques for dealing with it. The neo-conservative approach is not so historically relativist: it implies instead that the Soviet challenge is unique and irreconcilable. As Irving Kristol writes:

> The Soviet Union is governed by a Communist Party that has no claim to legitimacy other than that it is the bastion of anti-capitalism in a world not yet communist. . . . The continuing existence and prosperity of the US, along with that of the democracies of Western Europe, is a standing refutation of its ideological pretensions. . . . The leaders of the Soviet Union foresee its destiny quite clearly. If it becomes the world's dominant military power, all its other deficiencies will not count for much, whether abroad or at home. But if that ambition is frustrated, it is stalled in a blind alley, doomed to rust and decay.[7]

In other words, for reasons of *Soviet* structure and politics, the conflict between Moscow and Washington is not susceptible of mellowing or mitigation, but must end with the death or transformation of one or other of the two societies.

Some American scholars make a relevant distinction between an 'essentialist' and an 'opportunist' characterization of Soviet foreign policy: the first would hold (like the neo-conservatives) that Soviet policy was 'essentially' expansionist, the second (conservative) would hold that it was expansionist when opportunity was allowed. The third view, that Soviet policy is only 'defensively' expansionist, tends to be confined to left-liberal argument, and was therefore not exactly prevalent in President Reagan's Washington.

Another touchstone for distinguishing between the two positions may be found in Middle Eastern events. In the late 1940s, during the emergence of Israel as a sovereign state in President Truman's time, Israel was distinctly a Democratic cause, even a left-wing one. Soviet policy promoted Israel's emergence, in the interests of getting a British base removed from the Eastern Mediterranean, and the first substantial flow of weapons to the Israeli army in 1947–8 came from Czechoslovakia, with Soviet goodwill. Conservative opinion in Britain at the time was apt to see the newly-sovereign Israel as a Soviet pawn. Republican opinion in the United States was substantially pro-Arab, concerned about oil and military bases. The great turnabouts on these issues came with the Soviet decision in the mid-1950s that there was better diplomatic fishing on the Arab side of the Middle East's troubled waters. The consequent Soviet arms deal with Egypt in 1955 clinched the change. The highly articulate American-Jewish community from that time progressively provided more and more of the intellectual substance of neo-conservatism. That was why *Commentary* became the flagship of neo-conservatism.

Some of the earlier conservatism originating from the right-wing segment of the Eastern US Establishment had been traditionally quite anti-Semitic as well as anti-Zionist and anti-Israeli. Neo-conservatism's spokesmen have partially come from the East European Jewish Diaspora which fled to the United States from the Czarist pogroms of the late nineteenth and early twentieth centuries. So they have a historic grudge against Russians, as well as a contemporary one against the Soviet Union. In many cases, there is also the special bitterness mentioned earlier, arising from rejection of a previous radicalism, and perhaps a slight psychological edge of guilt as they contrast their own comfortable and prosperous situations in the US with that of their co-religionists whose ancestors went to Palestine from the same Diaspora and who now fight Israel's wars. And finally, there is the indignant resentment generated by the Soviet attitude on migration of Soviet Jews to Israel, and the barbarous treatment of the 'refuseniks'.

A lot of these distinctions crystallized during the trauma suffered by the American-Jewish community at the time of the 1973 Middle East war. The bitter attacks on Dr Kissinger by neo-conservative opinion during and after that war illustrate the differences between three right-wing positions rather neatly. A traditionalist conservative intellectual, serving a pragmatist Republican President (though he could equally have served a pragmatist Democrat and did indeed do some work for both Kennedy and Johnson) was not (though Jewish) squarely enough on the Israeli side to meet the requirements of the neo-conservatives.

Another context in which the differences between conservative and neo-conservative show up clearly is that of East–West relations in Europe. The prevalence of thoroughly conservative and traditionalist foreign-policy establishments in Western Europe during the Reagan years did not preclude the growth of a level of ill-feeling such that a Reagan neo-conservative policy-maker like Richard Perle could hint at an American move towards unilateralism, and one of the academic gurus of neo-conservatism like Irving Kristol could plug that idea openly. One might of course regard those ploys as mostly just heavy Washington signalling to coerce the Europeans into line on some immediate tactical question like levels of arms budgets or missile deployment, since no one with much sophistication in strategic doctrine, or any practical involvement in policy-making, could regard the demise of NATO (which is inherently probable in serious US unilateralism) as anything other than a devastating blow against Washington. (That is why the Russians have been working so hard to undermine NATO for forty years.) But the calculations of conservative *realpolitik* are sometimes hard for neo-conservatives to take, as was amply evident in the Kissinger years. (He was described as 'Spenglerian' and unAmerican by neo-conservative critics.) There may be little strategic logic to a unilateralist position, but adopting one, or threatening to, gives a good many Americans (right, left or centre) considerable emotional satisfaction when they are feeling particularly irked by some piece of European intransigence or criticism or heel-dragging.

In terms of the theory of foreign policy, one might say that the conservatives, especially the Europeans, continued to be consciously or unconsciously influenced by that very old maxim of European diplomacy: *cuius regio, eius religio*: that is, the sovereign gets to write the rules within his own domain. It was for centuries the basis for the ability of European states to live together: it conveys the acceptance as legitimate of governmental policies thoroughly repugnant to one's own values. And that implied a tendency to shrug off as of 'not our concern' the behaviour in domestic matters not only of the Soviet Union, but also of Third World societies like Libya or Nicaragua or, at the other extreme,

South Africa. The neo-conservatives did not see it that way, at least as far as left-wing regimes were concerned. Intellectually one could also make a case for unilateralist noises as a tactic to help Washington get its way in arguments within the alliance, or possibly as a serious policy option if the alliances should become actually hindrances rather than assets in American dealings with adversaries. Thus, many of the most interesting intellectual stances of the administration were developed in arguments with allies.

The intellectual and emotional background of the neo-conservatives gave them some sharp insights into political reality. However, it did not, over the long term, give them much in common with a relaxed and comfortable ex-Midwestern Californian of Irish Protestant background with a short attention-span, like Mr Reagan, despite his being very much a 'Hollywood poolside Zionist'. So the differences which developed in the later Reagan years were not really surprising. But for the first three years of Mr Reagan's first term, his declaratory signals – that is, mostly the Presidential rhetoric – were just about all that the neo-conservatives could have wished, and disguised from many people, especially outside America, the fact that the operational signals even then by no means matched them.

It will become easier to see this point if we look briefly at a cross-section of issues, contrasting the original rhetoric and the actual policy choices: that is, the declaratory and the operational signals. Though the Iran imbroglio offers a particularly clear case of Presidential credibility falling into the chasm between declaratory and operational policy, I shall reserve detailed examination of that to a later chapter, and for the moment use as examples China, Poland, the Korean airliner, Lebanon, the Gulf, and the gas pipeline. This chapter will look only at the contrast between words and deeds. The substance of policies will be examined later.

On China, the contrast is so obvious as hardly to need making. The early declaratory signals from the Reagan camp, especially before the election, had seemed to establish the President as a dedicated friend of Taiwan, prepared to risk disrupting the relationship with Beijing for the sake of the Chinese nationalists or for the sake of anti-communist consistency. In fact, in office President Reagan followed precisely the same path to the Great Wall as Presidents Nixon and Carter in their times, considerably stepped up the sale to China of advanced US technology, including sophisticated nuclear and avionics equipment, and even achieved the first US naval visit to a Chinese port since 1949.

In the Polish crisis, already under way when President Reagan came to office but reaching its decision-point only with the declaration of martial law in December 1981, the Reagan pattern hardly varied from that of US policy in other East European crises, established as early as the 1953 riots in East Germany when Dulles had just been installed in power. The rhetoric was vehement and the national debate expressed US outrage, but the actual sanctions against the Soviet Union were exceedingly mild. In particular, grain sales (on which President Reagan had already lifted the embargo which Jimmy Carter had imposed after Afghanistan) were not restricted, the Geneva arms-control negotiations proceeded, the US continued to participate in the Helsinki review talks, a meeting between Haig and Gromyko was allowed to take place as scheduled. In fact, aside from the suspension of Aeroflot services and some restrictions on high-technology exports, it is difficult to see anything in US operational policy which could have caused Soviet policy-makers to wince.

Washington's reactions to the shooting-down of the Korean airliner in September 1983 were almost a carbon-copy of those to the declaration of martial law in Poland nearly two years earlier. Again, the level of denunciation reached a new crescendo: again there were symbolic gestures of outrage – declaratory signals – such as denial of landing rights for Gromyko's plane when he sought to make his customary annual visit to the UN Assembly. But again, operational signals were quite otherwise. The grain deal was not rescinded. The Stockholm meeting (essentially a continuance of the Helsinki process which Mr Reagan had so often denounced in earlier years) was not only allowed to go ahead but was chosen as a venue for a low-key meeting between Shultz and Gromyko.

Lebanon, and the Middle East in general, offer a more complex pattern, but one of much the same basic meaning. Initially, the Reagan administration approach seemed to promise a policy with fewer efforts towards 'evenhandedness' than in Carter's time and thus more in line with neo-conservative urgings. Haig, in March 1981, told the Senate Foreign Relations Committee that the objective was to establish a consensus in the strategic regional sense among the states in the area, and in time this did eventuate in a strategic agreement with Israel, an objective of policy for neo-conservatives though a major irritant, of course, to Arabs. But in policy choices as a whole, during the Syrian missiles episode of April 1981, the Israeli bombing of the Baghdad reactor, the annexation of the Golan Heights and the initial phase of the Israeli invasion of the Lebanon in June 1982, the operational signals seemed to be rather of a tendency to leave the area in the hands of local actors. That stance was interpreted at the time, especially by pro-Arab European opinion, as advantageous in effect to Israel, but it did not in the longer term altogether work out that way.

The commitment of the Marines in August 1982 and the Reagan Plan initiative in September must, to my mind, be classed as strong declaratory signals rather than true operational commitments. When Eisenhower put Marines into the Lebanon in 1958 he used about 15 000 and left them there until the US objectives of the time had, for good or ill, been temporarily secured. The Reagan commitment of 1600 Marines, in contrast, was at a *token* level. They did not have a military purpose, but a diplomatic and political one: that is, they constituted a declaratory signal. When the Marines suffered the casualties of October 1983 the President declared that the United States had 'vital interests' in Lebanon. And the Secretary of State said: 'We are in Lebanon because the outcome will affect our whole position in the Middle East. To ask why Lebanon is important is to ask why the Middle East is important.' Those again were strong declaratory signals. But only a few months later, in February 1984, the Marines were simply taken out. Casualties, Congressional rough weather and the opening of election year added up to enough pressure to cause, in essence, the shrugging-off by the administration of an issue previously declared vital. So the operational signal – that Washington was leaving the control of events in local hands – remained the dominant one. The foreseeable advantage of these manoeuvres and ambivalences seemed over the longer term to accrue not to Israel, but to Syria. Lebanon, by the late Reagan years, appeared to have become a Syrian sphere of influence; possibly, indeed, an eventual province of Greater Syria. By that time the declaratory signals had been readjusted to match the operational signals: the Reagan administration, far from asserting more ambitious objectives than its predecessors in the area, appeared to be signalling itself content to leave events predominantly in local hands.

In the Gulf much the same pattern held good. Again the initial declaratory signals were strong. The Rapid Deployment Force was renamed the Central Command and fleshed out with assigned forces: carrier battle-groups and airborne divisions and fighter wings and such to a total (theoretically) of almost 300 000 men. But though a major war was in progress in the Gulf for almost the whole of Reagan's time in office, US intervention, even after the tanker-war was stepped up, was cautiously limited to helping secure the passage of oil cargoes, and exerting some pressure on Iran to accept a cease-fire without victory. It implied a tacit co-operative relation with a similar Soviet effort. The Reagan administration cultivated friends, like Oman, who would come in handy if push should ever come to shove in the Gulf, but the policy as a whole was kept low-key, showing deference to feeling among the Arab states, except for the arms deliveries to Iran which will be considered in a later chapter. On operational signals one would say that the US stance in the Gulf was a lot less ambitious than it would have been if the Reagan administration had been taking neo-conservative prescriptions seriously, and less ambitious indeed than the Carter doctrine had initially appeared to be. Obviously policy-makers were preoccupied with the alternative dangers of an Iranian victory or a marked increase in Soviet influence in the Gulf area, but the stratagems adopted to avert these risks stayed well below the threshold of major involvement against Iran.

The gas-pipeline showed an analogous phenomenon operating in an intramural crisis of the NATO alliance. The initial declaratory signals were, as on other issues, fierce: talk of sanctions against America's closest and most vital allies. And Washington did have a case: dependence by the West Europeans on Soviet sources for even a small proportion of their energy supplies did not seem a good idea. But the Europeans also had a case: their vulnerability to Middle East energy suppliers was so great that their general level of risk was not more than marginally increased by a small shift of energy dependence to the Soviet Union. Besides, they argued, giving the Russians in this way an additional stake in the prosperity and stability of Western Europe as a useful source of foreign currency might actually reduce the Soviet incentive to disruptive behaviour, even in the Middle East. And the Russians needed to be able to sell commodities like natural gas to the West if they were to buy Western goods in return. So the Europeans dug in their toes and shrugged off the Washington rhetoric. The gas flowed westward and hard currency eastward, though not in the quantities originally envisaged. US sanctions were not persisted in to any serious degree, and NATO therefore survived with hardly more than a scratch or two. Again, the contrast was between tough initial Washington declaratory signals and an eventual policy of shrugging the whole thing off.

These examples were not the only evidence, even during Mr Reagan's first three years of office, that though his rhetoric was originally with the neo-conservatives, his actual policies from the first tended to be conservative or pragmatic. The same inference might have been drawn from his major appointments in the foreign policy field. His two successive Secretaries of State – Alexander Haig and George Shultz – were both conservatives, and neither could have been mistaken for an ideologue. Of his six successive National Security Advisers, the first two, Richard Allen and William Clark, were comfortable, familiar aides, not universally applauded for the depth of their understanding of international politics. Their successors, Robert McFarlane and John Poindexter, proved (on the evidence of the Iran imbroglio) well out of their diplomatic depth in policy-making at this level. Frank Carlucci was an experienced professional, but soon was elevated to the role of Defense Secretary. General Colin Powell had only a brief stint in office, and by his time the President's capacity for diplomatic initiative was quite limited. Adding all eight foreign policy-makers together one would hardly come up with as clear and as well-deserved a reputation for combative skills in the US–Soviet conflict as in the single person of President Carter's National Security adviser, Zbigniew Brzezinski, or as much intellectual authority as Henry Kissinger. One might regard Jeane Kirkpatrick as initially the 'token neo-conservative' in the higher Reagan foreign-policy ranks, with her very visible (and audible) position as Ambassador to the UN. But the main point about that office is that its holder is strictly in the business of declaratory signals – oratory and votes. And, of course, not long after the declaratory signals went through their 1984 modification, Professor Kirkpatrick ceased to be the US voice at the UN. For a truly influential neo-conservative in a long-term policy-making position one had to move a rung down the security establishment ladder, to Richard Perle as Assistant Secretary of Defense for International Security Affairs until mid-1987. Arms control policy, on which his influence has already been much explored in other books, will be considered in a later chapter.

My argument may thus far only seem to be reiterating the point (now widely conceded) that the Reagan administration's bark was considerably fiercer than its bite, or to word it more theoretically, that the declaratory signals tended to be much sharper or more pugnacious than the operational ones, even in the cases of arms control and Central America which will be looked at in detail presently. But the argument proposed here is not just a historical point concerning the Reagan administration. It has implications also for the new set of decision-makers in Washington, and for the general theory of foreign policy. The basic question is whether the fierceness of the barking, so to speak, precluded the need for much in the way of biting, beyond, as it were, an occasional warning nip at easy targets like Grenada or Libya for purposes of demonstration of will.

If that were the case, switching our zoological metaphors, we could say that the superpowers (in relation to each other but not necessarily in relation to other members of the society of states) had reached the level of wisdom of gorillas in the equatorial jungle; each beating his own chest in the central clearing of his patch of territory, not as a prelude to battle, but as a preventative of the possible necessity of battle, these declaratory signals being the means of making it clear to his rivals how far he expected his writ to run, and that he was alert to resist encroachments on what he claimed as his domain.

It would probably be expecting too much, however, to assume such a degree of wisdom in those more dinosaur-like monsters, sovereign states. One of the few points of agreement between Mr Reagan's left-wing critics and his neo-conservative critics was the assertion that the contrary would prove the case: that is, that the loud declaratory signals were essentially ineffective or even counter-productive. Midge Decter, for instance, in the survey quoted earlier, remarked: 'It's worse to make thundering speeches and do nothing than to be quiet and do nothing.' The same sort of scorn was voiced by Garry Wills, from a liberal standpoint: 'Tough talk and retaliation are not the answer to our problem: they are our problem . . . we cannot afford tantrums.'[8] But there is a line of analysis which provides a theoretical rationale for the apparent evidence of the Reagan years that at least *temporary* success can sometimes be derived from a diplomatic technique relying heavily on loud declaratory signals.

To make this case, we must reflect on the concepts of capability, will, mood and 'atmospherics' in the relationships of the central balance, and particularly the signals which convey them. However, we must start by pointing again to the primary piece of evidence: the absence of any true crisis between Moscow and Washington in the Reagan years. True crises, as was argued earlier, must be defined as episodes in which the superpowers approach the brink of hostilities with each other, not episodes in which they are merely exchanging insults at rather above the standard rate. By that criterion, there was not even an approximation of a true superpower crisis in the years concerned. The nearest approaches were perhaps over the declaration of martial law in Poland in December 1981 and the shooting-down of the Korean airliner in September 1983. Some US commentators who should have known better (and did know better) used the word 'Sarajevo' in connection with the latter incident, but the mere mention of that name makes it clear how far the central-balance powers were then, in fact, from any actual warbearing crisis of that disastrous earlier sort: how far they were, indeed, from even *potential* warbearing crisis, of the style of Cuba 1962 or the various Berlin crises of the 1948–61 period. On those earlier occasions, one can say that central-balance hostilities were prevented by prudent crisis-management in a situation of alliance stability and overall deterrence. I shall look presently at the impact of the Reagan years on those three elements, which together make up the system which has successfully averted hostilities between the central-balance powers for more than forty years now. But the Reagan period, as far as the superpower relationship is concerned, must rather be characterized as one of apparent crisis-*avoidance*, precluding much need for actual crisis-*management*. And clearly, crisis-avoidance, if it can be practiced or induced, is preferable to even skilful crisis-management. A crisis in central-balance diplomacy is like a skid in freeway motoring: on the frozen roads of the Cold War such episodes may be highly likely, or even nearly inevitable, so those 'at the wheel', as it were, had better be capable of coping with skids when they do happen. But it is obviously preferable that a style of diplomatic driving should prevail which minimizes the incidence of skids. The evidence of the Reagan years seems to indicate that caution of that sort was somehow induced in central-balance relationships. That evidence was, of course, entirely at odds with the expectations in 1980–1 of the President's left-wing critics, who were given to freely forecasting war.

To understand why history fortunately did not match the more doom-laden prophecies, we must return again to the functions of declaratory and operational signals. Both sets of signals contribute to the expectations which the powers have of each other. Those expectations in turn are incorporated into the assessments of costs and risks which determine actual policy decisions on both sides of the central balance. But there is an important distinction between declaratory signals and operational signals particularly relevant to the Reagan years and the decade or two before them. The superpowers have for those thirty years or so had independent means of seeing for themselves, with the aid of satellites, overflights and sensors of various sorts, what the capabilities of the other side are. So the ambiguities from which have traditionally arisen the miscalculations that precipitate crises, and sometimes wars, are no longer in the field of relative capabilities. They are predominantly now in the field of will; sometimes the will of a society as a whole, sometimes the will of its dominant political élite, but more often the will of the chief decision-maker and the small group of policy-makers who immediately surround him.

And of that small group's will, in a situation of crisis, no satellite can provide direct observation. Operational policy does provide some signals bearing on will, but in this particular field declaratory signals – speeches and such – provide the most direct guide to mood, and thus cannot safely be discounted by an adversary as a signal of will. In other words, declaratory signals are a more important component of the total mix of signals now than they were before the age of surveillance (that is, before about 1960) because the remaining ambiguities of the power balance are mostly in the area of will rather than capacity, and declaratory signals tend to determine the image of will which each group of adversary decision-makers forms of the other. (Note that I do not say they convey the reality, only that they determine the image.)

One can perhaps demonstrate that point most readily by looking at the transition period between US administrations. Obviously, Soviet decision-makers did not have to make a new assessment of US capacities *vis-à-vis* their own society on 21 January 1981, but equally obviously they did have to make an assessment of the will, intentions and mood of the new decision-makers, an assessment which at that point in time would have to be based entirely on earlier declaratory signals, since the group concerned had not yet moved into operations.

With that analytical framework in mind, let us compare the operational and declaratory signals that came from Washington in the Carter years and in the Reagan years. The larger disparity was certainly between the two sets of declaratory signals. That is, the images of the two foreign policies, the ways in which the media presented them and in which adversary and allied decision-makers perceived them, certainly owed more to contrasts in what the two Presidents and their respective entourages *said* than to any vast differences in what the two administrations actually *did*. Indeed, it is rather difficult to think of many major operational differences at all, save the sharper and more combative stance during the Reagan years in the Caribbean and Central America, and the conspicuously greater early scepticism on arms control. (There is a case for putting arms-control proposals into the sphere primarily of declaratory policy anyway.) If one looks at the basic substance of most operational policies – continuance of support for NATO; continuance of a wary cultivation of China; continuance of support for Israel, along with as much or as little cultivation of Arab moderate governments as was compatible with the Israeli connection; a continuing consciousness that the security importance of Japan outweighed economic rivalries; continuing orientation to ASEAN and the Pacific especially in trade; a continuing restraint of the basic hostility of Vietnam and a certain ambivalence on Iran, detesting the Ayatollah's regime but not willing to push hostile feeling to a degree that would enable the Soviet Union to profit – on all these it is difficult to see more than marginal change.

Observing these continuities in operational policy (to which more examination will be given later) and contrasting it with the differences in media images and the differences also in the day-by-day international fortunes of the two administrations (especially for the first six Reagan years), it seems reasonable to conclude that the strong declaratory signals of the Reagan administration initially offset its somewhat ambiguous operational signals, and thus helped secure the basic objectives of policy, though at considerable costs which will be detailed presently. By contrast, in President Carter's time, the initial declaratory signals appear to have been counter-productive to his operational policies, to the sad detriment of his original hopes.

There is a Soviet policy concept which would neatly account for the reactions of the period among Moscow policy-makers: that of the 'correlation of forces', which though slightly different to the concept of the balance of power in Western neo-conservative and conservative doctrine, fulfils a similar function of policy guidance. On the overt Soviet reactions it appeared that the declaratory signals created by the Reagan rhetoric raised assessments in Moscow of the level of risk from Washington in any kind of 'forward policy'. Thus the 'correlation of forces', the central concept in most Leninist analysis,[9] would look less favourable. That conceivably inhibited even a probing or experimental venture into any such policy. It will be argued later that factors stemming from the Soviet side from 1981 to 1988 also militated against opportunity-snatching of the 1976–9 kind. So even a slight extra weight of assessed risk (created by US declaratory signals) could have proved significant enough to turn the scales. When scales are closely balanced, a feather's weight (or in this case, a few breaths of air) may serve to sway them.

There is indeed a piece of evidence from the cloak-and-dagger world of double agents to substantiate this thesis. The British had an agent called Oleg Gordievsky inside the KGB station in London during the early 1980s, and by his account, Soviet agents in Britain and elsewhere were told early in 1981, during President Reagan's first few months, to expect an American attack on the Soviet Union at any time. This intelligence alert was maintained until the end of 1983, Soviet agents being required to report everything of possible relevance, down to the limousine movements of senior officials and an effort to recruit blood-donors by the Greater London Council. On the timing, it seems clearly a Soviet reaction to the initial Reagan declaratory signals.

Central-balance war in the nuclear age is more likely to come from miscalculation than from deliberate challenge. Miscalculation, in the age of surveillance, is more likely to derive from uncertainties about the will of the chief decision-maker in the adversary camp, rather than the strategic capacities of the two systems. Khrushchev's apparent miscalculation about Kennedy offers an earlier analogy: he is reported to have come away from their Vienna meeting in 1961 convinced that the new young President was 'too liberal to fight'. The genesis of the Cuba missiles crisis, undoubtedly the most dangerous warbearing crisis of the entire nuclear period, may in part be seen in that assessment. Mr Carter (because of his declaratory signals) accidentally perhaps also engendered that same kind of miscalculation. Mr Reagan clearly engendered the opposite kind of assumptions: whether they too were miscalculations only came under debate during the final two years. The preservation of peace rests, unfortunately, on nothing more substantial than a system of expectations in Moscow and Washington as to how the decision-makers in the other capital will react in the event of unacceptable policies on their own part. So a central point of foreign policy must be to prevent any kind of under-estimate creeping into those sets of expectations. Thus Soviet reassessments, after the advent of Mr Reagan, must be accounted useful, rather than damaging, to the basic mechanism that keeps the peace, in the sense of helping reduce any dangerous tendency to discounting of risk, thus also reducing the chance of some lethal miscalculation.

And almost all done by words, one would say. So in a longer-term conspectus than is possible at present, the chief theoretical interest of the Reagan years, as a case-study in foreign policy techniques, may be of the importance of declaratory as against operational signals, image as against substance, words as against deeds.

2. 'Negotiation from Strength' Revisited

The most charitable of the interpretations offered earlier concerning President Reagan's foreign policy implied that its underlying strategy was 'negotiation from strength', an aspiration which had been made explicit, but not actually achieved, in US policy in the Acheson and Dulles periods: that is, the late 1940s and the whole decade of the 1950s. And it was further implied (more controversially) that the concept might conceivably have come rather close to realization in the middle years of the Reagan period, around 1984–5.

This chapter will explore those notions, especially the relevance to the Reagan years of the factors which caused the concept finally to come to nothing much in both earlier and later incarnations. It was downplayed (though never explicitly abandoned) as an aspiration during the difficulties of the 1960s and the détente of the 1970s. For the reasons why it reappeared so strongly in the Reagan period we must look at some parallels with the phase of history precisely thirty years earlier.[10]

An almost eerie similarity may be traced between 1981 and 1951, when the concept had had its previous most notable level of influence. In 1949, as in 1979, serious and respectable analysts had tended to see a phase of major danger about five years ahead, with a 'window of vulnerability' developing because of a perceived major change in the underlying strategic balance. In 1949 the reason was a true strategic milestone: the first Soviet atomic test. Along with the additional jolt of the Korean war in 1950, that was enough to induce a major Western countervailing reaction, an ambitious NATO arms build-up, US expenditure by 1953 reaching almost 15 per cent of GNP: more than twice the rate of the Reagan years. This US spending, like that of the Reagan period, was paralleled by rises in West European defence spending, never as high as that of the US, but much higher in the Eisenhower than in the Reagan years.

In the earlier period, as in the later, a potential technological 'quick fix' to restore an assumed-lost Western advantage also developed in the minds of policy-makers. Then it was the replacement of atomic weapons by nuclear ones: the second time around it was the 'SDI' or 'Star Wars' concept. The same fertile scientific mind, Dr Edward Teller's, was the father of both technological inspirations. So a powerful sense of *déjà vu* hung over the early 1980s for anyone who was once preoccupied with the early 1950s. Mr Gromyko, the only major policy-maker at more or less similar levels of influence in both patches of history, ought to have been particularly haunted by it because, on the first occasion as on the second, there was also a long-drawn-out Soviet succession crisis which affected his own personal fortunes. Then the succession was to Stalin, more recently it was to Brezhnev. Dulles then, like Reagan later, was given to heavy but not always convincing declaratory signals, as, for instance, the doctrine of 'massive and instant retaliation' enunciated in 1954. The marked change of tone in the Reagan declaratory signals during 1984 had perhaps no precise equivalent in Dulles's own time, but something similar happened in the final two Eisenhower years, with the advent of Christian Herter as Secretary of State.

The notion of negotiation from strength did not, of course, originate with Acheson and Dulles. Probably every diplomat in the three-thousand-year recorded history of the trade has been professionally conscious of the potential advantages of negotiating from whatever strength (or appearance of strength) his country can muster or contrive. Many of them, nevertheless, have had to make the best they could of a distasteful necessity to negotiate from weakness, as for instance after defeat in war. Some policy-makers for small powers have devoted considerable ingenuity to devising negotiating techniques suited to a permanent situation of relative weakness, and have achieved an effective diplomatic style of doing so. (Among the cruder techniques of this sort, the 'if-you-don't-support-me-I-will-collapse-and-where-will-you-be-then' ploy acquired a considerable popularity with Third World élites during the 1960s, *vis-à-vis* Washington. But unfortunately for weak regimes, as for instance the Western clients in Indochina before 1975, the effectiveness of such threats ceases when the domestic costs of supporting the threatened élite come to be seen as greater than the international costs of letting it collapse – a point relevant to the 'Reagan doctrine' which will be explored later. So a rather fragile and temporary feeling necessarily haunts even the most adroit practitioners of this particular diplomatic art-form).

On the whole, negotiating from strength is the preferred concept for every power whose policy-makers can possibly hope to bring it off: not only the United States and the Soviet Union but the former great powers of Western Europe, and potentially China or Japan. Thus, the aspiration itself should certainly not be regarded as unique to Washington, but it has been stated more explicitly as an intention by American policy-makers than by most others. Moreover, its failure to 'come off' has seemed more surprising in the American case, since the US has, after all, had from time to time a far more convincing edge of strength over 'all comers' than had been the lot of earlier great powers. And in the postwar period as a whole there have been considerable stretches of notable US ascendancy of strength *vis-à-vis* the Soviet Union. The reasons why that edge has proved diplomatically unusable offer illumination of the difficulties of foreign policy-making in the pluralist society. I shall return presently to the way those factors vitiated the aspiration during the first Cold War period, and the parallels implied for the Reagan period; but first, let us look at the way it re-emerged in Mr Reagan's time and is likely again to be reasserted in future despite whatever disappointments it may have created in the past. It is always reborn like the phoenix from the ashes of its last incarnation.

Basically, this persistence as aspiration is because the phrase ingeniously (and perhaps unconsciously for many of those who use it) combines appeals to the two basic orientations among the rather small segment of the population in any country which is attentive to discussion of international affairs. The usual estimate is that only between 5 and 15 per cent of the population in any country is regularly attentive to such discussions, so the most typical public stance on foreign-policy questions is inattention. But if we concentrate for the moment on the 10 per cent or so who form the 'attentive public', they will tend to be psychologically divided in various ratios for various countries between those whose orientation is towards 'strength', however defined, and those whose orientation is towards 'negotiation', with whatever objective. So the phrase 'negotiation from strength' manages to 'work both sides of the street', offering something to each group.

The optimists, whose conscious or unconscious premise is that international conflict is mostly based on specific, resolvable disputes or misunderstandings, and that harmony of interests is the true international 'normality' which would prevail if only such obstacles to peace were removed through discussion ('summit' or otherwise) can focus on the 'negotiation' part of the phrase: negotiation will produce accommodation, and ultimately international harmony and peace. On the other hand, those whose temperament is more pessimistic, or whose intellectual conviction is that international conflict, not international harmony, is the normal condition of international politics, especially as between rival superpowers of opposed value-systems, can concentrate on the 'strength-building' part of the concept: there may eventually be negotiations, but those negotiations will merely register or formalize a situation of fact. So 'summitry' or other modes of discussion are tolerated with a shrug rather than greeted with enthusiasm, or with any strong belief that they will change things. It is held to be in reality the preliminary process of strength-building that will or may change the actual relationships of international politics. The negotiations which follow, and the agreements which may come out of those negotiations, merely provide the society of states with notification of the changes. They register the facts created by the new 'correlation of forces', in the Soviet phrase.

However, in situations of crisis or drama (such as summit meetings) the 'big battalions' of the usually-inattentive majority of the population will tend to swing in one direction or the other, partly according to the atmospherics of the time, but with a bias in favour of the conventional wisdom in their society concerning international politics. And in the United States that conventional wisdom is still more or less Wilsonian-progressive: that is, diplomatic effort towards the harmonization of international interests is still basically taken to be desirable, whatever the prevailing official rhetoric as to the intrinsic unalterable clash of values with the adversary.

That was strikingly clear from the public opinion polls taken in November 1985 just before the first Reagan–Gorbachev meeting.[11] The summit meeting was rated a good idea by 82 per cent of the voters: only 6 per cent thought it a bad idea. And that approval was despite considerable pessimism about any undertakings that might emerge from the meeting: 66 per cent did not believe that Soviet decision-makers could be trusted to keep to any bargain that was struck, and 28 per cent (with what might be regarded as either surprising cynicism or refreshing realism) did not believe that American decision-makers could be trusted to keep to their bargains either. The overall trend of American opinion on the Soviet Union during the Reagan years was shown to be apparently rather at odds with official exhortations. In 1980, towards the end of Jimmy Carter's term, only 45 per cent of Americans had been détente-minded *vis-à-vis* Moscow. By 1985 the proportion had jumped to 65 per cent. Likewise, the proportion of Americans who believed that the Soviet Union represented a very serious threat to the US dropped from 52 per cent in September 1983 to 32 per cent in November 1985.[12] So in effect the alarmist Reagan rhetoric of the first three years had not, in fact, created alarm, or not of a lasting sort, at least in the US. (Among allied and non-aligned opinion it created alarm and disapproval, directed mostly against the US rather than the Soviet Union).

For the US the more robust image, created rather by the President's declaratory signals than by any truly significant change by that date in existing capabilities as between the two powers, had reduced the number of Americans who saw the Russians as a serious threat from more than half the population to less than a third, and had thus increased the proportion regarding it as by then 'safe' to enter negotiations. In other words, and in one of the more notable of the many paradoxes of this patch of foreign-policy experience, a Presidential style of rhetoric that had emphasized strength-building had produced a greater popular tolerance of negotiation, simply by promoting renewed national self-assurance.

The working-both-sides-of-the-psychological-street aspect of 'negotiation from strength' as a diplomatic aspiration, however, camouflages a more subtle reason for its perennial popularity. That is, that it blends the well-known concept of 'deterrence' with the more esoteric notion of 'compellance'. 'Deterrence' only aims at inhibiting the adversary from decisions you do not want him to take, by credibly conveying that you have both the power to impose heavy penalties for unacceptable behaviour and the will to actually do so. 'Compellance' is a word invented by political scientists to convey a more ambitious idea: not just to prevent the adversary from doing something that you do not want but to make him do something that you *do* want; take his troops out of Afghanistan, for instance, or allow full powers of independent decision-making to other members of the Warsaw Pact, or dismantle the SS–20 missiles in Eastern Europe. The reason why the notion of compellance is less familiar than deterrence is that it had not until recently come to anything much, though it had done so in the old days of the unequal treaties. To my mind, there are insuperable psychological and political factors which are likely always to limit its use in the nuclear age. But there is undoubtedly a specious hint of the prospect of compellance, not merely deterrence, in the overtones of the concept of negotiation from strength. Various critics, in fact, argued that there was more than a hint of compellance aspiration in the Reagan policies as a whole. I would amend that somewhat by saying that there were indeed overtones of compellance, but they were confined to the declaratory signals, at least as far as the central balance was concerned. (One would obviously make a different judgement on, for instance, Nicaragua and perhaps Libya.) The distinction is however rather hard to demonstrate, since the policies involved tend to be ones in which official statements are almost inevitably couched in terms which strive to convey an impression rather more formidable than the reality of operation policy would warrant.

The most obvious example is the Strategic Defense Initiative. As of 1988, the SDI could hardly be regarded by either its most enthusiastic proponents or its most fervent denouncers as anything more than an ambitious research programme. Their attitudes to it were governed entirely by what they hoped or feared would come out of that research programme during the next two decades. For the decision-makers in Moscow, judging by their reactions, it had undoubtedly constituted an alarming declaratory signal, interpreted as saying: 'We are working on some technologies that may make your vast investment in land-based ICBMs just so much money down the drain, by potentially foiling their capacity for nuclear strike. What is more, once we get our prospective shield in place, we might be less inhibited about using our very powerful sword of offensive capacity during a crisis. So you will need to be careful you do not provoke us.' That was indisputably a very traumatic set of ideas for Moscow, but it was still just a statement about the possible future balance of forces: that is, a declaratory signal. Nothing operationally effective is up there yet, and many very eminent Americans and other Westerners (including possible future official ones) have rushed to tell Soviet decision-makers that there is never likely to be. So in total the signals which have gone to Moscow on this matter have been confused and contradictory, but they have practically all been declaratory. As with other forms of investment in military research, there is, of course, an implied understanding that the notion will move from declaratory to operational effect at some unpredictable future date; but obviously not within the Reagan years, nor probably the Bush years, especially given the official downgrading of expectations concerning the projected system in the first few Bush weeks. So from Reagan's first mention of the subject in March 1983 until his final months of office, what was in operation was just a massive but ambivalent set of declaratory signals, the unofficial ones mostly saying 'It can't be done', the official ones saying 'It can be done'.

And yet these merely declaratory signals, on the evidence, seem to have constituted in one respect a surprisingly effective approximation to a basis for 'negotiation from strength', judging primarily by the changes of Soviet stance in the arms-control negotiations. Those changes will be discussed in more detail in a later chapter. Meantime, the reasons why Soviet policy-makers appeared to have been taking the Star Wars idea more seriously than many eminent American authorities are worth examining.

First, let us note that there were two quite different visions or concepts of a potential strategic defence for the US, or the West in general. There was the Utopian or science-fiction vision which pictures a sort of impermeable translucent 'astrodome' over the whole country with incoming missiles bouncing harmlessly off it. 'Protecting us from nuclear missiles as a roof protects a family from rain', as the President put it in July 1986. That version was sold officially in television discussions and such. The second version, which is a great deal more feasible even on present or presently-envisageable technologies (and which some experts said might be in operation by the mid-1990s), was a 'high-tech' update of the existing modes of strategic defence, through a 'multi-layered' system which would protect specifically America's land-based nuclear strike capacity, and thus in effect *reinforce* rather than supplant the present technique of deterrence, by strengthening it at its one point of theoretical weakness. (That point of weakness is the very faint but not inconceivable prospect of success for a Soviet pre-emptive strike at US land-based missiles, plus a 'blackmail' ploy to avert the otherwise inevitable US retaliatory strike.) Such a less ambitious system would *not* have to be impermeable to be effective. Even a 50 per cent 'kill-rate' against incoming missiles would so lengthen the odds against success for pre-emptive strike as to rule it out for any rational decision-maker. There are various ways of making a case against even this more feasible but less ambitious version of the SDI, including the argument that it is an inordinately expensive way of securing such slight extra safety as it might provide, and that the retaliatory mechanisms and other factors which already discourage any Soviet decision-maker from contemplating pre-emptive strike remain overwhelmingly strong even without it. That particular debate will be examined presently. Here we are concerned with just the apparent Soviet reason for taking a different view from that prescribed by many Western sceptics concerning SDI.

Much authoritative Western comment has, for instance, implied that Soviet policy-makers could saturate any feasible American strategic defences merely by multiplying their present stock of offensive missiles. But as Stephen Meyer, as eminent Sovietologist and Pentagon consultant has pointed out,[13] the Russians could for various reasons feel obliged to try an 'emulating' as well as an 'offsetting' response. The SDI was not seen in Moscow as merely raising the offence–defence balance another notch in quantitative terms: it was seen as the initiation of 'a new type of arms race, one involving previously unknown new types of weapons based on new physical principles'. The Soviet Union would be provided with an actual *advantage* by SDI if offsetting it were so easy a matter of stepping up missile or warhead production lines as some Western critics alleged. If that were true, it would make the intensive Soviet effort at blocking the project rather surprising. But in reality the Russians remain at a marked disadvantage in the most salient technologies of the proposed concept, which are those of target acquisition, tracking, sensors and, most especially, computer hardware and software. Micro-miniaturization, advanced electronics and fine-tolerance engineering are areas in which the Soviet Union lags a long way behind the West and Japan. If Soviet policy-makers decided to try and catch up in these fields of special skills, they would have to start investing heavily in the necessary technologies at once. But there are many other areas of much simpler technologies also crying out for investment in the Soviet economy, like the demands for consumer goods and conventional kinds of machine-tools. Investment in those areas will obviously have far more immediate political and economic pay-off than investment in the very sophisticated technologies necessary for an emulative response to the SDI. The level of sacrifice imposed on Soviet society for the upkeep of the existing military machine was already far higher than the equivalent burdens in any NATO country. Allocating yet another one or two per cent of GNP, on top of the present 14 to 17 per cent allotted to Soviet defence, for either an emulating or even a less expensive offsetting response to SDI was therefore the last thing Mr Gorbachev was likely to want.

Furthermore, Soviet strategic assumptions and Soviet experience actually magnified the US proposal in ways which may have made it seem more formidable from Moscow than from the Western capitals. On the strategic assumptions assumed to lie behind the proposal, Soviet standard military doctrine teaches that a strategic defensive move must be linked with a strategic offensive concept to conduce to victory. Therefore, Soviet analysts were more likely than Western ones to see a coherent strategic offensive design behind the defensive shield that President Reagan kept talking of. On the Soviet view, a shield is only meaningful because it allows more prospect of using the sword. That is a point on which ironically (and perhaps unconsciously) many of the Western *opponents* of SDI also were actually magnifying the impact of the concept for Russian policy-makers, since they likewise tended to argue that the idea made sense only as an offensive rather than a defensive technique. (The argument is that if either superpower wants to secure an option of pre-emptive strike, the logical first move is for it to construct itself a shield to take care of those of the adversary's missiles that it is unable to take out in the pre-emptive strike. Otherwise the effort at pre-emption would be almost certain to prove suicidal.)

A further factor was the high prestige, not to say apprehension, that US technology commands in Moscow. Soviet policy-makers have good reason to know that formidable outcomes are likely when an American collectivity of many scientists and technicians is bent towards a chosen task. That judgement does not rest merely on the recent examples of the Manhattan project, the moon landing and the development of anti-satellite systems. Soviet policy-makers have had a history of finding themselves obliged to import US technology (legally or otherwise) ever since Lenin's time, starting with car plants and tractors. Gallingly for them, there seems as much of an American edge in 1989 on fifth-generation computers and such as there was in 1919 on Model T Fords. Yet whatever the costs incurred in pursuing the new generation of advanced technologies, it remains the case that the capability of the Soviet armed forces (not economic efficiency, ideological appeal or human welfare and freedom) is the one basis for Soviet claims to parity with the other superpower. Soviet decision-makers thus will not readily let that claim be tarnished by failure to compete at the 'leading edge'. Nor do powerful leaders of the armed forces in any country readily content themselves with anything less than 'state-of-the-art' technology in their weapon-systems. There is also the point that, owing to the different structure of strategic nuclear capacity on the two sides, with Soviet capacity mostly land-based, an equally effective SDI on both sides would still adjust the odds more in US favour.

So in effect one might argue that the 'Star Wars' speech represented at least a notable piece of serendipity on the part of Mr Reagan. Political luck or intuition provided him with just the kind of project most likely to put his Soviet opposite number into a corner out of which he might decide to negotiate his way by serious concessions. And that appears to have been one factor in producing the sequence of Soviet manoeuvres in the arms-control field which will be examined in a later chapter.

Reverting to the general notion of 'negotiation from strength', one must regard some other sets of declaratory signals as complementary or supplementary to the SDI proposal, as efforts to convey an image of strength, but of a more immediate sort, affecting the present rather than the future. The concepts I have in mind are the 'Lehman doctrine' or maritime strategic doctrine in naval matters, the 'follow-on-forces attack' (FOFA) in NATO's contingency plans, along with the 'air-land battle' doctrine of the US army, and (in conflicts affecting the Third World) the 'Reagan Doctrine'.

The 'Reagan Doctrine' will be considered in much more detail in a later chapter looking specifically at the Third World policies of the administration. Here it is enough to say that its implication, in brief, was that a Communist victory in a Third World country would no longer (if it ever had been) be regarded as necessarily history's last word on the matter: communist regimes, like any other variety, can be toppled by a new turn of the political wheel. Furthermore, it was heavily hinted, American policy would be dedicated to at least oiling the wheel to see if it could be turned. Thus, one could define the 'Reagan doctrine' as, in intention, a claim to repeal the 'Brezhnev Doctrine', at least as far as Third World societies were concerned, though not for Eastern Europe. The 'Brezhnev Doctrine' is, of course, a Western phrase (firmly repudiated by Soviet spokesmen), for the implication that seemed to emerge from the Soviet Union sending its tanks into Czechoslovakia to repress the 1968 outbreak of freedom there. The assumption, derived from a sentence in one of Brezhnev's own speeches at the time, was that the Soviet Union would not let any country 'won for socialism' (that is, under Soviet control of an enforceable sort) ever again quit the communist camp, even if its people obviously wanted to. The same principle had appeared to be implied in the 1979 decision to send Soviet troops into Afghanistan. But it was a considerable extension to imply that the Brezhnev Doctrine would be maintained not only in Eastern Europe (where it had been more or less tacitly acquiesced in, without the actual name, since 1953), but also, where feasible, in the Third World. 'Where feasible' is, in fact, the operative word for the concept as a whole in both its earlier and its later incarnations. Obviously, it could not have been applied without enormous costs during China's break with Moscow in 1959–60. Even during Yugoslavia's departure from the communist camp in 1948, the costs of military action to put down Tito's presumption looked too high for that cautious Soviet decision-maker Stalin. But since then it has been applied both in instances where the Soviet stake is very high (as in the remaining *glacis* in Eastern Europe) or where the costs and risks seemed likely to be relatively low, as was, at least initially, apparently deemed to be the case in Afghanistan. The Reagan doctrine may, therefore, be considered mostly a ghost in the mirror, a pale reflection of the Soviet claim with the signs reversed. Its level of operational as against declaratory success will be examined in a later chapter, dealing with the Third World policies of the Administration.

The 'Lehman doctrine', or maritime strategic doctrine, as

deduced from the speeches principally of Reagan's initial Secretary for the Navy, John Lehman, and Admiral James D. Watkins[14] appeared to signal that the 580-ship, 14-carrier-group US Navy, whose coming into being had been almost secured by the late Reagan years, would be used in a tactical offensive mode in the event of general war, being 'surged' towards areas of concentration of the Soviet Navy (like the Barents Sea, the Sea of Okhotsk, the Sea of Japan) in the hope that Soviet ships and submarines could be 'bottled up' or destroyed. The 'follow-on-forces-attack' (FOFA) concept in NATO, along with the 'air–land battle' doctrine for the US Army similarly implied taking any war into adversary territory, rather than waiting for the attack in Western territory.

Putting these assorted concepts together, the Western doctrines adopted or publicized during the Reagan period (some of which had actually been developed well before then) signalled – consciously, deliberately, assiduously signalled – a far more pugnacious or 'hairtrigger' stance *vis-à-vis* the adversary than had been conveyed by earlier Administrations, except perhaps during the Dulles period. The 'horizontal escalation' associated with the maritime strategic doctrine was quite clearly a 'dusting off' of the old 'massive and instant retaliation at places of our own choosing' concept put forward in a 1954 Dulles speech. But they were all primarily declaratory signals. Again paradoxically, it was left to the Secretary of Defense to supply the corrective 'small print' with the 'Weinberger Doctrine' of November 1984, which conveyed, to the contrary, that US combat forces would be carefully and prudently used, such use being officially regarded as a 'last resort'. And in *operational* policy it was undoubtedly the Weinberger Doctrine that prevailed. US land forces were engaged in armed combat during the Reagan years only against the tiny Cuban contingent in Grenada, about 650 members of a construction corps. One cannot get operationally much more cautious than that. US air forces in the Libya strikes were deployed against whatever could be mounted by Soviet air-defence systems manned by Libyans: again, not exactly a high-risk operation. The US Navy certainly had some of its units put in harm's way during the convoying of reflagged tankers in the Persian Gulf, but again at quite a cautious level. Even 'covert' forces, of a heavily-publicized sort, as in Nicaragua, seem to have operated as much in the media as in the combat zones.

The point at issue for this chapter, however, is whether declaratory signals considerably more combative or pugnacious than the accompanying operational signals did, in fact, conduce to the overall strategic objective of negotiation from strength. A final verdict for the Reagan years on that issue must be very tentative until a little more perspective has been provided by the lapse of a year or two. The only clear case seems to be in arms control, an area in which the longer-term effects of policies are often at odds with their initial apparent meanings. However, re-examination of the factors which vitiated similar ambitions in the Acheson–Dulles period suggested that success was inherently always unlikely.

The root impediments to the achieving of such policy objectives, as was implied earlier, must be seen as deriving from the general nature of decision-making in a pluralistic society. Doubly pluralistic, in fact, for not only is the US itself a pluralist democracy in which many disparate voices must be allowed their say in policy-making, but also its decisions have to be meshed in with those of the Western alliance, a whole cohort of pluralistic democracies, even the smallest of which (like Denmark) has at least some minimal influence on the process of alliance decision-making.

During its earlier trial-run, both elements of the 'negotiation from strength' concept proved far more difficult to put into practice than to formulate in theory. On the 'negotiation' side, the optimum phase, in the sense of the phase when Western diplomatic leverage appears in retrospect to have been higher than at any earlier point or any later point to date, seems to have been more or less missed. Looking at the 'correlation of forces' as nearly as possible from a Moscow perspective, the months immediately after Stalin's death in March 1953 appear to have represented the true Soviet post-war 'low'. The surviving members of the initial collegiate leadership which inherited power were lucky to have escaped with their lives during the terrible paranoid last months of the old tyrant. Their relations with each other were still tentative: Beria was shot because the others found him too dangerous. The Soviet economy was still close to its desperate postwar nadir. An atomic bomb had been tested and work was frantically proceeding on a thermonuclear device, but the first test of that was still some months away, so the outcome remained uncertain. There was no bomb stockpile, no effective means of delivery, no Soviet 'blue-water navy', no missile capacity, an outmoded air force. Even the Soviet alliance structure apparently looked unpromising when seen from Moscow. From the first, Mao's China seems to have been regarded with more suspicion than enthusiasm both by Stalin and Khrushchev, judging by the account in Khrushchev's memoirs. A series of riots in East Germany had indicated how tenuous the Soviet hold was in eastern Europe, and the 'show trials' of the next couple of years indicated how strained was the loyalty of the East European leaderships to the new leadership in Moscow which did not inspire the same degree of terror as Stalin.

By contrast, the West seemed during that patch of history to have settled into its stride. US expenditure on arms was at its postwar peak, about 15 per cent of GNP, and the other NATO powers were also spending heavily for arms. There was in fact a 'prescribed level' of 10 per cent for the major NATO powers, and Britain had even exceeded it at about 11- per cent, figures that would not even have been contemplated in Europe during the Reagan years. The ambitious Lisbon goals for NATO's conventional forces had been announced, and it was not yet clear that they would be missed. An American nuclear bomb had been tested in November 1952 and word of its awesome performance was beginning to seep out. The American advantage in means of delivery was still overwhelming. The deployment of West German troops in the NATO line was foreshadowed. The Communist challenge in Korea had been successfully beaten off, Japan had been recruited into the American alliance structure. The Marshall Plan had fostered a remarkable Western economic recovery which was still gathering force. The US political system had just installed in office as President the most renowned Western general of the Second World War, who was also an ex-Commander of NATO.

In the light of all that, the shaky new Soviet leadership could hardly have failed to be deeply conscious of how unfavourable for the time being the correlation of forces had become. Even Stalin in his final year of life seems, in fact, to have been preoccupied with the adverse prospects, for his last negotiating bid *vis-à-vis* the West, an offer of German reunification in exchange for neutralization (made in a note of 10 March 1952, almost a year before his death), probably represented the largest potential Soviet territorial concession in Europe in the postwar period. The level of Western advantage, and hence the potential for negotiating leverage, seems in retrospect as if it should have been abundantly clear at the time. Moreover, a consciousness of that point had been signalled from the other side, especially in some of Malenkov's statements. Yet the moment was somehow missed. Why?

In Washington the new set of decision-makers of the Eisenhower administration were still settling in to their first year of office. Though Dulles, both while Secretary of State and during his earlier long campaign for that office, was given to rather loud declaratory signals, like the 'massive and instant retaliation' speech of early 1954, he was to prove basically a very cautious man when it came to operational policy. For instance, when the riots in East Germany broke out early in 1953, looking just like the opportunity for a 'liberation' or 'rollback' process such as he had been talking about right through the Presidential electoral campaign, he did precisely nothing – setting the precedent followed by the West right up to the Reagan policy in the Polish crisis of 1981–2, of taking no risks during phases of overt dissent in the Soviet sphere of power.

But there were other reasons, especially from the part of the European decision-makers. The French were at the time embroiled in a phase of double anguish: over their declining military fortunes in Indo-China (the final defeat at Dien Bien Phu was only a year away) and over the European Defence Community (EDC), a scheme unfortunately ruined by being introduced long before its time. It aimed to create a genuinely integrated European army, though at the sacrifice of national armies. The need not to disrupt the chances of that plan (and then when it fell apart to find a substitute for it), absorbed most of the energies of the entire NATO diplomatic establishment from 1952 to 1955, and made them reluctant even to contemplate anything (such as negotiations with the Russians) which would distract attention from the EDC struggle.

The one conspicuous exception to all these failures of historical intuition among the policy-makers of the time was Winston Churchill, who began to talk of the desirability of a meeting with the 'new men in the Kremlin' almost as soon as Stalin's funeral was over. In the first Commons debate after that event, in his remarkable speech of 11 May 1953, he urged a conference 'without long delay . . . on the highest level . . . of the smallest number of powers and persons possible . . . not overhung by a ponderous or rigid agenda or led into mazes or jungles of technical details zealously contested by hordes of official drawn-up in vast and cumbrous array' so that nothing 'should as it were supersede or take the emphasis out of what may be a profound movement of Russian feeling'. 'It would be a mistake', he said 'to assume that nothing could be settled with Soviet Russia unless or until everything is settled.'

But providence and history seemed to fight against this diplomatic initiative during the two years which elapsed before actual agreement on a meeting. Churchill himself suffered a slight stroke a couple of months later, which diminished his hold on his party and government and marked the beginning of the end of his tenure of office. Dr Adenauer was not convinced that the optimum moment had arrived, and neither were the French. In Washington it was still high noon for Senator Joe McCarthy who saw all such proposals as products of the Communist conspiracy: he was still able to be an embarrassment even to Dulles and to terrorize the State Department. He made one of his most offensive speeches in the Senate debate on the matter. Even Churchill's own Cabinet seemed to be signalling a belief that the 'old man' had gone overboard. (Nye Bevan said that the Prime Minister's trouble was that 'he was trying to ignite a lot of wet flannel round him'.) So nothing much came of the idea in 1953, and thus the brief moment of optimum Western leverage passed. By the time of the Berlin Conference, in January 1954, the Soviet leadership was beginning to 'get its act together'. A few months later, in the May Day parade, new Soviet long-range bombers (Bison, Badger and Bear) were beginning to be shown off, declaratory signals that the imbalance in delivery systems could be redressed. Presumably the Soviet nuclear stockpile by then was beginning to grow, the first successful test having been held a year or so earlier. By 1955 Khrushchev had more or less consolidated his ascendancy over the rest of the collegiate leadership, and his original rival, Georgi Malenkov (who had seemed the most peace-orientated of them) was dispatched to run a power-station. Two years further on, with the launching of the first Sputnik in 1957, the Russians managed, in effect, their opening bid to be taken seriously as technological rivals of the US, and Khrushchev by then was well launched on his campaign to undo Western power in the Third World, a project to which Stalin had never seemed to give much attention. The visit to India in 1955, the Egyptian arms deal also of 1955, the explicit threat to Britain and France over Suez in 1956, the hectoring rhetoric in the Middle East crisis of 1958, the beginnings of the connection with Cuba after Castro's victory in 1959, the ambitious (though successfully frustrated) policy in the Congo crisis of 1960, and the bold decision to end the drain of manpower westward by building the Berlin Wall in 1961: all these were milestones on the upward trend of Soviet diplomatic self-confidence from its nadir in 1953. One might argue that this initial resurgence of Soviet power crested to a fall in the Cuba missile crisis of 1962, and that another brief phase of Western ascendancy (or at any rate, sense of ascendancy) supervened in 1963, but it was very brief and became totally lost with the deeper American embroilment in Vietnam a year later.

The mid-to-late 1960s seem, in fact, the period in which the West probably passed the 'point of no return' as far as restoration of its once advantageous strategic edge *vis-à-vis* Soviet power was concerned. On the one hand, the decision-makers in Moscow worked hard at creating effective rocket and naval forces after the lesson of Cuba. On the other hand, the Washington decision-makers spent not only American military resources but American domestic moral and political authority, along with alliance cohesion, in the effort to win the lost and strategically unjustifiable battle in Vietnam. So that by the time the Nixon policy-makers came to office in 1969, Washington had fallen to almost as low a point in relative diplomatic leverage as Moscow had been at sixteen years earlier. In the circumstances, Dr Kissinger played the very unfavourable hand that history had dealt with considerable skill, creating a phase of détente and a rearrangement of the central balance. The Carter years saw a recovery of domestic morale, but American self-confidence in diplomacy suffered further wounds then because of Iran and the hostage crisis.

Thus it was not until President Reagan's time that the international context of the American bargaining position *vis-à-vis* the Soviet Union began to look even moderately favourable again. President Reagan was initially lucky in his moment of history, not only compared to his three immediate predecessors in Washington, but also compared to three of his successive 'opposite numbers' in the Kremlin. For Andropov and Chernenko were in office too briefly to be anything more than part of the succession crisis between Brezhnev and Gorbachev. That obviously changed with the advent of Mr Gorbachev, whose impact on the diplomatic contest between the superpowers will be discussed in more detail in the next chapter. But here it must be said that if the optimum negotiating period from the point of view of the West passed as briefly in the mid-1980s as it had done in the early 1950s, the reasons in both cases owed as much or more to developments in the US as to anything that had happened in the Soviet Union.

In late 1986 President Reagan's diplomatic and political luck temporarily deserted him: he seemed indeed to cram eight years bad luck into his penultimate year. Neither domestically nor internationally was he later able to regain his earlier leverage. The Democratic recapture of the Senate in November 1986 would in any event have cast the 'lame duck' shadow over his final years, but 'Irancontragate' and an extraordinary number of other things (like the great Wall Street crash and the Supreme Court nominations) seemed to come apart in his Administration's hands at about the same time.

So at the present retrospect, it seems reasonable to argue that the year from late 1984 to late 1985 represented the nearest approximation to an optimum negotiating period that can be discerned during the Reagan years. The President had been returned to power with an overwhelming majority: his party had control of the Senate though not the House of Representatives: his popularity was at an all-time high: most of his major allies had governments sympathetic to his foreign policy drives. The national mood was buoyant and self-confident, American technology seemed all-conquering, the defence budgets were at their peak.

A number of milestones show the steep descent from that brief high point. First, the Gramm-Rudman-Hollings amendment put a question-mark over the future of the defence budgets. Then the Challenger disaster put a question mark over the technology. But the prospects still seemed reasonable for most of 1986, until the steeper plunge downward from November, with the Congressional elections and, of course, 'Irancontragate', and in 1987 the Wall Street crash. The parallel with the earlier period is again clear in the brevity of the period of advantage; about a year in both the early 1950s and the mid-1980s. The mutability of political fortune in pluralistic democracies being what it is, that span of time may, on the historical evidence, be the most that can be expected.

One distinction between the two parallel phases of US foreign policy, however, is that during the first, the early 1950s, the territorial boundaries of the adversary blocs in Europe still seemed subject to negotiation. That is, there still seemed a hope of negotiating the Soviet Union out of Eastern Germany, and Stalin's note of March 1952, of course, played deliberately on that prospect. Until the late 1980s, no such prospect revived, and the true subject of negotiation was simply the strategic balance between the Western and Soviet blocs, though this was slightly camouflaged by assorted declaratory signals about human rights and regional disputes. Crisis stability through arms control had become the dominant issue in the superpower debate.

It is possible to argue that (on that one subject) President Reagan was in 1987–8 still able to muster a certain amount of strategic strength or diplomatic leverage which showed in the final negotiations, during his time in office, with Mr Gorbachev. But many other factors went into that phase of US–Soviet relations, and they will be examined in the next two chapters.

3. Getting Along with Evil Empires

I implied earlier that to many of Ronald Reagan's numerous left and liberal critics, one of the most puzzling aspects of his years in office was the almost total absence during that time of true crises between Washington and Moscow on the one hand, or Washington and Beijing on the other. That was in contrast, during the early years, with the ample supply of abrasive rhetoric, at least between Washington and Moscow, with the Russians giving as good as they got in the polemical line. For every mention of the 'evil empire', there was at least equivalent Soviet air-time dwelling on resemblances which Soviet spokesmen laboured implausibly to detect between Ronald Reagan and Adolf Hitler. But to reiterate the point that true crises must be defined as periods when the central-balance powers are in danger of approaching the brink of hostilities with each other (not periods when they are merely trading insults at rather more than the standard rate), on that criterion there were no such episodes between 1981 and 1988. Thus, examination of the dichotomy between the rhetorical 'overkill' of, especially, the first three Reagan years and the operational caution (on both sides) of the whole period strengthens the case for arguing that the international polemics may have had 'safety-valve-and-warning-signal' functions which possibly reduced the chances of actual blow-up. But other substantial reasons for the absence of true crises will be adduced in this chapter.

Relations with China are deliberately considered here alongside those with the Soviet Union, because diplomatic calculations in all three capitals – Washington, Moscow and Beijing – ever since the first Kissinger visit in 1971, have had to take into account the triangular element in the central balancing process. Some decision-makers have been more inclined than others to talk openly of 'playing the China card' (or 'the America card' or 'the Soviet card') but all have been conscious that there is an inescapable objective advantage to the situation traditionally described in

European diplomacy as that of the 'balancer' power – that is, the one most easily able to shift its position *vis-à-vis* other members of the central balance, and thus dominate or restrain their policies. Britain enjoyed and profited by that situation for centuries in the old European balance. In the Washington–Moscow–Beijing relationship, China has seemed fully aware, judging by its adroit diplomatic signals, that it might ultimately hope to secure some similar advantages through international manoeuvre.

Mr Reagan's phrase about an 'empire of evil' was, of course, specifically applied to the Soviet Union, but from either a conservative or a neo-conservative point of view China was, if ideology alone had to be taken into account, originally the more rebarbative of the two powers. Its most violent period of social upheaval, the Cultural Revolution, was much more recent (1966–76), and presented a much more dramatic picture of revolutionary destruction than anything that had happened in the Soviet Union since 1917. The reason for American *rapprochement* in the Nixon–Ford–Carter period with Beijing rather than Moscow derived from balance-of-power pragmatism: 'the enemy of my enemy is my (potential) friend'. Only marginal interests of the United States were then or are foreseeably likely to be vulnerable to Chinese power. But truly vital interests were and are vulnerable to Soviet power. So the government in Beijing, even if it had remained as wholeheartedly revolutionary as it seemed in the mid-1960s (which it did not), had logically to be regarded as a 'subsidiary' enemy for the United States: the Soviet Union was the real focus of immediate danger. And the same logic inspired, for parallel reasons, Beijing's judgement that the Soviet Union rather than the United States was the more truly dangerous adversary of its own society, despite its ideology. So Beijing and Washington each had cause to see the other as potential 'co-belligerents' if not potential allies, in containing the spread south and east of Soviet influence in Asia and the Pacific. Especially, of course, after the Vietnamese government, America's most recent enemy and China's most irritating one, became also Moscow's protégé.

Thus there was always a good pragmatic case for Mr Reagan to spare China much in the way of moral rhetoric, and to direct his blasts principally at the Soviet Union. On the other hand, just before his inauguration, Mr Reagan in a *Time* interview had said that China was 'a country whose government subscribes to an ideology based on a belief in destroying governments like ours'. He had suggested that the 'unofficial' relations with Taiwan be elevated to official status, and had attacked the Carter administration's agreement on normalization of relations with China. The issue of the sale of military equipment to Taiwan was already on the agenda from the late Carter period, since sales had been resumed in 1980 and Beijing had then made its objections clear.

Yet even during the inauguration ceremony there was a signal that the forces in Washington making for continuity of policy would prevail over the ideological pressures to reverse it: the representation of Taiwan was kept to non-official level. The Carter normalization communiqué of 1978 was reaffirmed in February 1981, and when Haig visited China in June of that year he announced that the Reagan Administration would contemplate even the sale of lethal weapons to Beijing.

These Reagan Administration concessions did not, of course, ease all the frictions. The question of military equipment for Taiwan continued to be a constant irritant throughout the Reagan years, as it had been earlier; and there were others: restrictions on the sale of US high technology equipment of various sorts, especially nuclear and military, and protectionist barriers against Chinese textiles and other goods in American markets. Between 1981 and 1983 the relationship often seemed headed for the rocks, but it never quite got there and moved into quieter waters after the Reagan visit to China in April 1984. In the last two Reagan years some shadows were cast over this situation by Chinese arms sales and some domestic political ups and downs in China, but the cordial relationship was solid enough to last his time, and into Bush's.

One would have to say, however, that most of the reasons for this relative harmony in place of expected discord (which surprised the more alarmist prophets on both left and right in America) lay primarily with the chief Chinese decision-maker, Deng Xiaoping, and his notion of China's priorities, rather than with Mr Reagan and his understanding of American strategies. The role of 'great helmsman', in succession to Mao Tse Tung, was not firmly in Mr Deng's hands until about the time of Mr Reagan's smoother inheritance of the American helm in 1981. Even after the fall of the 'Gang of Four', other factions of the Chinese leadership with other priorities retained the capacity to restrain Deng's course of action, even though he was able to retire some unconvinced comrades in the 'old guard', of which he was, of course, also a member. To the end of the period, covert opposition to his policies remained, especially (according to some Sinologists' opinions) within the armed services. Nevertheless, by the middle of Mr Reagan's first term it appeared likely that Mr Deng's priorities for China would remain the dominant ones at least for the remainder of the Reagan years. That provided a fortunate way out of potential dilemmas for the Reagan policy-makers, since these priorities and assumptions fitted usefully into Washington's hopes of China.

The chief danger of true crisis would have been if the dominant Chinese decision-makers had assigned a high or early priority to the reintegration of Taiwan into China, and had appeared to be contemplating a solution through military means. That was not, perhaps, very likely even before reassertion of Deng's ascendancy in policy-making, since Mao himself had told Dr Kissinger in the earliest days of the *rapprochement* that China was prepared to wait a hundred years if necessary for reunification. Moreover, the kind of military equipment that Beijing's forces would have needed to conquer Taiwan by armed force (substantial quantities of air and naval equipment of advanced types) might have been impossible to acquire within the Reagan years even if the decision had been made to pursue that objective. But what was reassuring about Mr Deng's China, from Washington's point of view, was the operational indication that any such enterprise had been put off to the indefinite future.

That was conveyed as much by the Chinese negotiations with Britain over the future of Hong Kong as by any other signal. There had been, ever since the early 1970s, a hope among analysts that the problem of future Chinese irredentism on Taiwan would be eased by what had been called the 'one China, two Hong Kongs' solution. That is, that the decision-makers in Beijing, once they had reckoned up the costs of any effort to reintegrate Taiwan by armed force (costs which would have to be estimated in terms of diplomatic frictions with the US and military opportunities for the Soviet Union, as well as the costs of the weaponry, the actual casualties in battle and the possible swathe of destruction both sides of the Taiwan Straits) would opt instead for an impressively liberal-seeming settlement on Hong Kong, with the hope that, over the years, watching the city flourish would constitute an inducement to Taiwan's decision-makers to choose a similar pathway. That, of course, may not be likely to happen while the present generation of 'mainlanders' (headed, however, by Lee Teng-hui, who is Taiwan-born) holds power on the island. But they are old men now, and the Hong Kong settlement (which promised fifty years' tolerance of the colony's entrepreneurial capitalist economy after the hand-back of the territory in 1997) was intended to see out their sons' and even their grandsons' time. Only after the crisis of June 1989 in China did the longer-term prospects arouse international disquiet. So the 'one country, two social systems' principle applied to Hong Kong in the settlement reached by Beijing with Britain's Mrs Thatcher in 1984 in fact offered a way down from an uncomfortable hook for all three of the capitals concerned. It gave Beijing's decision-makers a rationale for leaving things much as they were for the indefinite future on both Hong Kong and Taiwan, in order for the 'reassuring example' technique to work. It allowed Britain to plan a graceful retreat from one of the final relics of empire without having to fear an immediate collapse, since Beijing would be interested not only in preserving Hong Kong's prosperity for the sake of the foreign exchange it brought in and as a model for other economic zones of China, but also as an experiment which Taiwan would be watching with fearful anxiety. There was already a brisk trade between Taiwan and the mainland, conducted via Hong Kong because of the official Taiwan ban on direct trade, and if it were to be preserved some further *rapprochement* would have to be made by the time of Hong Kong's reversion. Finally, of course, the settlement was a bonus for Washington, diplomatically speaking, because it appeared to consign to the distant future (long after the Reagan and Bush years) any chance of hostilities in the Taiwan Straits. Even Hong Kong itself, if matters had gone wrong and a serious row had erupted between Britain and China, could have provided painful embarrassments for Washington, as in the case of that other left-over relic of empire, the Falklands.

The goals set for China by Deng Xiaoping – the 'four modernizations', with primary concentration on modernizing the economy – might conceivably have been advanced by some *rapprochement* with the Soviet Union, and that always had to be contemplated as a possibility by the Reagan policy-makers. Every now and then the Chinese signals seemed to indicate that it was about to happen, usually when Washington, from Beijing's point of view, seemed less than co-operative on some issue or other. Moreover, as soon as Mr Gorbachev was well settled in power, he began to indicate (especially in his Vladivostok speech of 28 July 1986) that the general tone of Soviet diplomacy *vis-à-vis* China was likely to become much more flexible and conciliatory than it had been in his predecessors' times, right back to and including Stalin. Yet Sino–Soviet rapprochement did not get very far in the Reagan years. Of the three Chinese requirements for better relations – Soviet exit from Afghanistan, Vietnamese relinquishing of Cambodia and a pull-back of some of the Soviet troops in the vicinity of the Chinese border – the Russians seemed by 1988 to be offering concessions on the first and third, and possibly on the second, as Vietnam indicated plans for exit from Cambodia. However, Soviet policy in the Pacific seemed to be in an expanding phase, with bids for influence among the small Pacific island states. So the Chinese had (on balance) until the final Reagan year, almost as much reason to feel 'encircled' by Soviet forces as they had eight years earlier, though that feeling was no doubt mitigated by Mr Gorbachev's more flexible and adroit diplomacy. Soviet troops or Soviet allies were still on their Northern and Central Asian frontiers, and also for the time being in Afghanistan, Cambodia and Vietnam. With Vietnam, indeed, Soviet ties seemed to be strengthening, and Soviet naval and air deployments increasing: reports had pens for Soviet submarines under construction in the old American base at Cam Ranh Bay. All that gave the Chinese excellent balance-of-power reasons for adhering to their connection with the US, despite such irritants as the continued US sale of weaponry to Taiwan. So Mr Reagan's Washington was, for several years, relieved of the prospect of major crisis in a useful diplomatic relationship, which also held some economic promise of a distant sort.

The low priority assigned by Mr Deng to defence modernization – it ranked last in the list of four – was of slightly ambivalent significance to Washington: reassuring in that it seemed another clear signal that China did not expect to solve any of its problems by military action in the foreseeable future (a signal strengthened by Mr Deng's decision to demobilize a million men, which was good news for Taiwan, obviously), but also a signal that made China look less immediately formidable to the Soviet Union and Vietnam. Beijing may pose serious military problems to the decision-makers in Moscow some time in the twenty-first century, but not within Mr Reagan's years or those of his immediate successors.

On balance, however, its chief implication was that both the operational and the declaratory signals of the Reagan period could the more uninhibitedly be directed to convey a firm adversary stance towards Moscow, bluntly, consciously and deliberately to reverse the earlier Carter implications that Washington would be less preoccupied with that particular adversary relationship. The initial Reagan rhetoric certainly pulled no punches, and had a simplistic quality, a sort of verbal Rambo-ism:

> Let's not delude ourselves, the Soviet Union underlies all the unrest that's going on. If they weren't engaged in this game of dominoes there wouldn't be any hot spots in the world.[15]

> The only morality they recognize is what will further their cause: meaning they reserve unto themselves the right to commit any crime, to lie, to cheat . . .[16]

Yet, as was noted earlier, all was rather quiet, save on the reciprocal rhetorical front, even in the first three Reagan years. As in the case of China, some of the reasons obviously stemmed from the other side of the verbal confrontation. President Reagan's first term in office comprised the final months of illness and decline of Brezhnev, the quasi-interregnum as his death visibly approached, the brief survival of President Andropov, and the few months in office of another ailing veteran of the Politburo, President Chernenko. That is to say, the decisions made in Moscow during those four years were those of men who (less sprightly than their elderly opposite number in Washington) all had good reasons to be conscious of their own mortality. Despite a few exceptions like the Ayatollah or Ho Chi Minh, elderly, ailing men are not on the whole usually given to adventurous foreign policies. One could also argue that not only were the decision-makers in Moscow exceptionally elderly and all below par in health during the Reagan first term (so that one might on that basis alone have expected a certain 'immobilism' in Soviet policy) but also that the Soviet policy-machine had too many existing problems on its hands to take the sort of initiatives which might have created more. Afghanistan and Poland and the needs of useful allies in Cuba and Vietnam and South Yemen and Iraq and Syria and Ethiopia appeared to have left few resources even for marginal and faltering allies in Angola and Mozambique, much less for the taking on of major new commitments. (What was sent to Nicaragua and El Salvador via Cuba could hardly be so regarded.)

One might also argue that the domestic difficulties of the Soviet sphere of power, largely the results of economic failures, imposed their own constraints. Or, less optimistically, one could say that there is visible in Soviet policy an alternation, accidental or deliberate, of periods of 'forward policy' (as 1976–9) and of relative pause while the gains of that forward policy are consolidated or digested. (Rather in the manner, symbolically enough, of the polar bear which pursues a vigorous predatory policy while the sun shines, and retires to live off that intake during less favourable seasons.) On that interpretation, the comparative quiet of the first Reagan term could have been seen as a natural consequence of Soviet activism in the Carter years. Reagan, in other words, then enjoyed the good fortune of Carter's bad fortune. But on that analysis the relative immobilism of Soviet policy would have had to be regarded as a short-term phenomenon, not necessarily likely to persist for more than a few years.

With the advent of Mr Gorbachev in March 1985, the 'elderly ailing decision-maker' syndrome obviously vanished from Soviet policy-making. But the economic impediments to more adventurous policies remained, and probably even became stronger. As many Sovietologists have pointed out, Mr Gorbachev, more decidedly than his predecessors, was committed from the first to a costly long-term programme of economic and social reform, and needed arms control to justify a reduction of Soviet defence budgets in the interests of the domestic changes he hoped for. So he did, in fact, call for a revival of détente immediately on accession to office, and began also a 'PR' campaign of personal visits to endow the Soviet Union with a more reassuring image in Europe. He visited London in 1984 and Paris in 1985, 'warming up', so to speak, for his encounters with Mr Reagan in 1985, 1986, 1987 and 1988. His diplomacy at the Geneva, Reykjavik, Washington and Moscow summit meetings and in the arms control proposals was strikingly adroit and imaginative. President Reagan had obviously at last met someone in his own league as a 'PR' man. The barrage of Soviet global initiatives indicated the underlying strategy: getting tension a bit lower and so impressing world public opinion (especially European opinion) with the new flexibility of Soviet policy.

Gorbachev had good reasons to put a major personal effort into Soviet diplomacy, for on almost all the factors which go into Moscow's own estimates of the 'correlation of forces' (in his time as earlier, still the basic guide to international policy in Marxist–Leninist analysis) the balance had shifted against Moscow in the six years or so before he entered office. The roots of the troubles, primarily economic and social, seemed so deeply embedded in the Soviet system as to be likely to defy extirpation without major political upheaval:

> The present economic system cannot deliver the sustained expansion without which Soviet power will falter. It cannot create and assimilate the new technology or command the high labor productivity without which intensive growth is not possible. Declining growth rates have limited the availability of new capital. The cost of extracting natural resources has skyrocketed; there are labor shortages; the Soviet machine-stock is the oldest of any industrial power. Few incentives are available to stimulate labor productivity and technological progress. The system of centralized direct planning stresses quantity over quality and lacks the flexibility necessary for innovation. The backward infrastructure of industry, construction and agriculture produces enormous waste.
>
> ... The Soviets have always proclaimed that the contest with capitalism would be decided in favour of the system best able to secure high productivity and speedier technological progress. According to this test, capitalism has virtually won.[17]

These problems did not, of course, necessarily mean that there was no possible scope for Soviet adventures in foreign policy. Decision-makers faced with intractable troubles at home have often looked to distractions abroad as a mode of offsetting them. But in the Reagan years (which Mr Gorbachev presumably hoped to regard as only the 'first act' of potentially a long career as chief policy-maker in Moscow, stretching, if he remains successful, almost into the twenty-first century) there was no sign that his mind was turning in that direction. Very much the reverse signal was assiduously conveyed: in the words of Seweryn Bialer, the 'effort to avoid dangerous confrontations that would divert energy and resources from domestic revitalisation' seemed a major factor in his policy.[18]

Clear indications were given from the outset that Mr Gorbachev intended to be his own foreign and defence strategist and that some of the 'old hands' who had exerted decisive influence for many decades would suddenly become less powerful. Mr Gromyko, the embodiment of Soviet diplomacy from Stalin's time, was 'kicked upstairs' to the ceremonial duties of the Presidency and after the amazing party congress of June 1988 eventually retired as a backbencher. Anatoly Dobrynin was brought back from his important Washington post as Ambassador to the still more important 'backroom boy' function of head of the International Division of the Secretariat, an appointment whose power and prestige would be enhanced by his previous status of candidate member of the Politburo. That obviously was a visible signal of concentration on the US relationship: Mr Dobrynin's expertise was in the Washington policy process from his many years in that city, and he had shown over that time his own considerable talent for 'PR' *vis-à-vis* American audiences. As foreign secretary, Mr Gorbachev appointed Mr Shevardnadze, who had little earlier foreign-policy experience, and would thus (unlike Mr Gromyko) inevitably be seen as 'Gorbachev's man'. (One might see an ironic parallel between the relative positions and qualifications of Shevardnadze and Dobrynin, respectively, as advisers to Mr Gorbachev with those of Rogers and Kissinger as the Nixon foreign policy team: a 'front man' who would be seen as a personal choice and a 'backroom boy' of known intellectual resource. Perhaps Mr Dobrynin had been impressed by that set-up and recommended a parallel arrangement to his boss. Mr Shevardnadze survived much better than his American exemplar, however.) Mr Gorbachev also managed to 'sideline' not only his own earlier rival, Grigory Romanov, but the formidable Marshal Nikolai Ogarkov (appointed to a major theatre command that placed his HQ well away from Moscow at Minsk) and later Marshal Akromeyev. Thus as long as he maintained a general ascendancy over his Politburo colleagues, there seemed no reason to envisage much serious competition for him as a maker of Soviet security policy.

Soviet foreign relations at the time of Gorbachev's arrival in power were not in much better shape than economic prospects. The Soviet Union had suffered one of its sharpest defeats of the whole postwar period with the NATO 'two-track' decision of 1979, which proposed deployment of intermediate-range missiles in Europe. Moscow's most strenuous diplomatic efforts in the Reagan first term were concentrated on securing reversal of that decision, but the endeavour was a resounding failure. Even the most wavering among the NATO allies, the Netherlands and others, despite all the pressures of their peace movements, stuck to the 1979 decision. Soviet political appeal and leverage in Western Europe appeared visibly in decline. The once-powerful Communist parties of Italy, France, Spain and Portugal had become mere shadows of their earlier selves. Even in Greece, the radical government in office had been far less damaging to NATO than was earlier predicted. In the Third World several marginal allies (Angola, Mozambique, Libya) had fallen into considerable trouble. The postwar wave of zeal for left-wing prescriptions for national advance appeared subject to doubt everywhere: the forces of the market were newly respectable even in Communist societies like China and Hungary. The Soviet involvement in Afghanistan at the time still dragged painfully along without resolution, damaging relations with all Muslim states. Even the merits of advanced Soviet weapon-systems came under critical scrutiny as the results of military encounters in Lebanon, Syria, Libya were reckoned up by strategic analysts.

Mr Gorbachev's leadership seemed at first merely reformist, in the waging of campaigns against alcoholism, corruption and general slackness in the bureaucracy and the economy. So his changes, unlike those made by Mr Deng in China, appeared not initially radical, and perhaps his position within the Politburo until towards the end of the Reagan period still remained provisional or tentative enough to make radical measures infeasible, even though he may have wanted them. By the last few Reagan months, more genuinely transformatory changes were clearly his objective. Their future potential impact on American foreign policy, assuming he remains in power, will be considered in the final chapter.

Since the relationship with the United States was on the whole ambivalent and confusing during the Reagan years (despite its central and crucial importance), Moscow's most hopeful original tactical concentration was on other powers, following the logic of the indirect approach. The Soviet peace offensive won more applause in Western Europe and Japan than in the United States: Reykjavik in particular caused a good deal of subdued initial dissension in NATO, though there was a skilful US 'damage-limitation' campaign afterwards. Arms control agreements were offered to Britain and France, closer economic ties to the EEC as a whole. Overtures were made to Beijing, especially in the Vladivostok speech of July 1986, and Shevardnadze was sent to visit Tokyo. But during the Reagan period, the Gorbachev diplomatic initiatives tended to stop short of radical change. Japan was not offered back the Northern Territories. China got no immediately decisive concessions on its three conditions for a more cordial relationship, though it did get a better deal on the delimitation of its river boundaries with the Soviet Union, the clear prospect of a Soviet exit from Afghanistan and possibly a Vietnamese exit from Cambodia.

The Reagan years in American foreign policy must obviously be regarded as, on present probabilities, perhaps only the beginning years of Gorbachev as a maker of both foreign and domestic policy for the Soviet Union. On the indications of 1987–9, that was a hopeful but at the same time a formidable prospect for the Western alliance as a whole, and for the United States as its leader in particular. Assuming that his enemies and rivals in the party élite are not able to cut short his career, and that some at least of his reforms prove successful, the Soviet Union towards the turn of the century may as a result of his efforts be a more efficient society. But will that necessarily make it a less dangerous one? It is a fallacy to assume that a more open society at home must mean less ambitious Soviet objectives in external policy. The opposite might well be the case: Khrushchev in his time set the fashion for Soviet inner-circle candour in his secret speech of 1956 about the crimes of the Stalin era, but imprudence on his part created the Cuba missile crisis of 1962, which the Russians themselves agree was the most dangerous crisis of the nuclear age. Gorbachev appears on course to be equally candid about the Brezhnev era, but no one can be certain on the evidence to date that he will stay in office, or prove as steady and cautious a decision-maker in the external relations of the Soviet Union as the world needs if it is to survive an approaching dangerous transition in the nuclear age. Mr Reagan's famous luck served him to the last in one respect, in that his 'opposite number' in the Kremlin as he approached the end of his term of office was one as orientated towards arms control as Mr Gorbachev appeared to be from 1986 to 1989. Perhaps it served him even better in that the Soviet Union he had to deal with had not as yet had time to gain much advantage, economically or diplomatically, from the sort of changes Mr Gorbachev seemed to be setting in motion.

4. Arms and Arms Control: A Reversal of Signals

Probably the loudest declaratory signal from the Reagan camp during the struggles for nomination and election, and from the Administration during the first years of office, was of the necessity of swift American rearmament, and a firm rejection of any earlier 'conventional wisdom' that arms control agreements as such should be regarded as in the same sacred category as motherhood and apple pie, or should be construed as necessarily of benefit to the United States or to the prospects of peace. The 'Committee on the Present Danger', which had raised a most effective banner against SALT II, was influential in the administration, and its founder, Paul Nitze, was the chief initial arms-control negotiator, and remained a very influential one. The still more influential Richard Perle, well-known as an intellectual sceptic of the historical usefulness of arms-control treaties, was obviously in an excellent position to make his views effective as Assistant Secretary of Defense for International Security Affairs until mid-1987. So the Administration was at first expected by both its friends and its critics to be notable for a substantial arms build-up and little or no progress on arms control.

Probably that general area of policy was, in fact, the one in which the declaratory and the operational signals most nearly matched each other, at least during the first three Reagan years. The candidate had said he would raise defence allocations, and he did: he had indicated solid doubt about several existing arms-control measures and no enthusiasm for new ones, at least for the time being. And there were in fact no arms-control agreements during the first Reagan term. The formal arms-control proposals put forward in 1981 and the negotiations at Geneva and Vienna seemed well enough to deserve their appearance of being for intra-alliance reasons primarily, and to a lesser extent to placate critical US opinion.

On the other hand, even in this area of policy, there was still some mismatch between the popular image (especially outside America) and the reality. For instance, the strongly (even ostentatiously) signalled picture of a rapid overall increase of US armed strength, a picture that the peace movement, especially in Europe, tended to describe as 'the greatest arms build-up in history', was never precisely that. The original financial figures seem at first sight to indicate that it might have been: arms budgets were initially (before Gramm–Rudman–Hollings) postulated at $183 billion for 1982, $209 billion for 1983, $239 billion for 1984, $278 billion for 1985, $315 billion for 1986, $346 billion for 1987, and $377 billion for 1988. But one has to look also at another set of figures, those for the actual or postulated military establishment, and there the Reagan build-up seems at first sight surprisingly hard to find. The Navy, which did the best of the services, progressed triumphantly almost to attain its long-standing 600-ship target, including fifteen carrier-groups, but a large number of the keels had been laid down before Mr Reagan entered office. (Necessarily so, since a major naval ship takes more than eight years to build.) And the Air Force got approval of the B–1 bomber, as well as more rapid progress on the 'Stealth' technology, which might someday negate Soviet advantage in air defence. But in the most-debated field, land-based strategic nuclear missile capacity *vis-à-vis* the Soviet Union, the initial implication that the Reagan Administration would make a determined effort to outdo both the Russians and the Carter Administration was not fully sustained in experience. President Carter had proposed to build 200 MX missiles and to base them in some mode that would make them invulnerable to a Soviet pre-emptive strike. No agreement was ever reached on what that mode would be, but the project did represent an ambitious effort to wipe out the Soviet edge in land-based nuclear strike capacity within a few years.

By the final year of the Reagan Administration, no such ambitious objective appeared to be within measurable distance of achievement or was any longer to be sought. About fifty MX missiles (renamed Peacekeeper) had been deployed, fifty more had been authorized, but doubt had begun to be voiced concerning their accuracy and reliability. There was a project for mobile-basing in rail-cars, but that had not come to anything within the Reagan years, and was uncertain for the Bush years. In the meantime, the basing-mode was in the old Minuteman silos which had previously been scorned as too vulnerable. The future of the once-favoured alternative, the mobile single-warhead Midgetman, appeared very uncertain (it had many Pentagon critics), though a strong friend in Brent Scowcroft, President Bush's National Security Advisor, and some aspects of the 1987 arms-control proposals seemed to indicate it as eventually a logical choice. A mobile deployment was contemplated in its case also. The US stock of nuclear warheads was built up and modernized, substantially to increase the proportion with 'hard-target kill capacity', that is for use in a counterforce mode. The Trident D–5 submarine missile represented a quantum leap in capacity for precise nuclear strike based on a near-invulnerable platform, but that project also predated the Reagan period. Moreover, all such ballistic weapon systems were subject, after Reykjavik, to some very large question-marks concerning the long-term future, as schemes for reducing this whole category of delivery-vehicles within ten years (or by the end of the century) came under apparently serious discussion.

In strategic warhead numbers, the 'ballpark' estimates current at the time of Reykjavik put the two powers on essential parity, at about 11–12 thousand each: more precise estimates such as those published by the International Institute for Strategic Studies suggested about 10 716 Soviet and 12 846 American warheads on long-range delivery systems (launchers were put at 1910 for the US and 2502 for the Soviet Union).[19] In short- and intermediate-range ballistic missile warheads, on the other hand, substantial advantage in numbers remained with the Soviet Union. But the United States had the edge in aircraft and cruise missiles, and in qualitative matters like accuracy and survivability. At the end of Mr Reagan's term, as at its beginning, it therefore seemed reasonable to describe the US–Soviet relationship in this most crucial field as 'asymmetric parity' or 'essential equivalence'. American procurement of both strategic and theatre nuclear warheads was, however, much faster in the Reagan years than it had been in the Carter years. On land-based conventional forces and battlefield weapons like tanks and artillery in Europe, the numerical advantage remained with the Russians, though overall the situation continued to be rather closer to a relatively stable and viable balance than was usually pictured in US official statements. The Soviet edge was real, but not substantial enough to make attack a reasonable risk.

So, it may be asked, what precisely did the Reagan arms build-up achieve? What precisely was the extra money spent on? Part of the answer is, of course, that the contemporary arms race is qualitative rather than quantitative. The money went partly on research and development for the new weapon-systems (B–1, 'Stealth', 'Midgetman', D–5, SDI) which, except for the B–1, had not yet entered the inventory in substantial numbers (or at all) by 1988, but which might radically alter the balance of forces by the early or mid-1990s. Since the average 'lead-time' for new weapons-systems is ten years (and much longer for radically new systems like SDI) even a president who gets two terms is essentially, in his defence budgets, mostly building assets or problems for his successor. Another part of the answer is that a good deal of money went to provide better pay and conditions for members of the armed forces, and that this did show relatively prompt results in terms of quality of personnel, recruitment rates and re-enlistment rates. A third part of the answer is that, much less usefully, a great deal of money also seemed to go on the process known as 'gold-plating' equipment: making it ever more elaborate and expensive, sometimes at the sacrifice of numbers, sturdiness and workability on the actual battlefield. The inability, apparently, of the Pentagon to overcome this tendency (as exemplified, for instance, in the $7000 aircraft coffee-maker and other scandals, as far as the public was concerned) was a substantial factor in rapidly undermining the original 1980–1 consensus for the ambitious defence budgets. Its serious aspects were in advanced weapon-systems like the B–1 bomber and various kinds of missiles, guns and vehicles. Once it was assumed that the arms race with the Soviet Union must be essentially qualitative rather than quantitative, 'high-tech' solutions were inevitably seen as the answers to military problems. But the sacrifice of quantity for 'quality' (or often apparently for elaboration and sophistication) held great dangers, even aside from the swollen procurement costs.

The least noted but most important part of the reason for the contrast between the projected defence budgets and the relatively unspectacular change in actual numbers (as against quality) of both men and weapons in the defence establishment was that the almost universally-held picture of an unprecedentedly large transfer, during the early Reagan years, of US national resources to military purposes was never entirely accurate in the first place.

The astronomical size of the originally projected budget figures rather disguised the fact that by the fairest measure for historical and international comparison, which is proportion of GNP spent on defence, the Reagan build-up was at roughly half the rate of the initial Cold War rearmament of the Truman–Eisenhower years.

In 1953 the US had spent almost 15 per cent of GNP on defence. Though that admittedly was during the Korean war, even in a year of peace and détente, 1955, the figure was still 11 per cent. The originally projected rate of expenditure during the Reagan years was 7.5 per cent of GNP But the actual average rates, dropping in the final year to 5.9 per cent, stayed overall about 6.1 per cent, a proportion that had often been reached or exceeded during the previous four decades. Moreover, since arms spending imposes a greater level of real sacrifice at lower national income levels (just as spending 7 per cent of family income on insurance would impose a greater burden on a relatively poor family than a relatively prosperous one) so the higher proportion of GNP spent on defence in the Eisenhower years (when both nominal and real national income was a great deal less than in the Reagan years), represented an even higher level of real sacrifice (comparatively speaking) at the earlier period than the figures seem to indicate. The widely-held assumption that the Reagan expenditure proposals were vastly higher than those of the *late* Carter period was also somewhat mistaken. In his final budget, Jimmy Carter had proposed an increase in defence spending of 47.6 per cent for 1981–4. Though the initial Reagan proposals upped that to 58.6 per cent, the actual increase was 43 per cent. But the stereotype of the Carter period remained dominated by an arms-reducing image, created originally by his having said as a candidate that he hoped to cut 5 to 7 billion dollars a year from the arms budgets he had inherited. Public images, once established by the characteristic 'overkill' methods of the contemporary media, seem to become practically impossible to dispose of.

Indeed, one might say that Mr Carter and Mr Reagan were each, according to one's point of view, a victim or a beneficiary of assumptions about their records on arms procurement that owed more to media 'hype' and to their own declaratory signals than to substantial real differences in their strategic objectives (other than on SDI). Mr Carter came to office with the image of an earnest well-meaning friend of arms-control, and an enemy of inflated arms spending, and that image stayed with him even despite the final rise in his actual arms budgets and the sharp right-turn in his last year on many foreign and defence policy issues. Mr Reagan came to office with the image of a dedicated sceptic on arms-control, and a determined rebuilder of US military muscle, and that latter image likewise stayed with him until the final years, even though, for instance, he had continued for six years to observe the (unratified) SALT II Treaty that Mr Carter had signed, and even though his actual arms budgets were by no means beyond the historical norm for the United States in the postwar decades as a whole.

That last statement requires amplification and justification, since it is so at odds with most people's assumptions about the matter. When one looks back over the whole four decades (1948–88) from the early years of the first Cold War to the end of Mr Reagan's second term, American spending on armaments must be seen to have reached a clear peak of almost 15 per cent of GNP in 1953 (under the joint influence of the Korean war and the first rearmament phase) and declined gradually to a fairly firm plateau of 5 to 7 per cent of GNP over the following three decades. During what right-wing critics sometimes called the 'decade of neglect' (1970–80), the figures did occasionally fall a little below 5 per cent: 4.9 per cent in 1977, 4.7 per cent in 1978 and 1979. The revulsion in American society as a whole during that decade against war and militarism and overseas adventures (the 'Vietnam syndrome') inevitably had an effect on Congressional and public attitudes to arms budgets. So the rate of expansion of defence budget authority in the early Reagan years was by contrast initially very high. But when the budgets are assessed as a whole against the general trends for the postwar period, the average for the Reagan years is somewhat *below* the average for the previous two decades, 1960–80, which was 7.3 per cent of GNP. If one uses as a basis for comparison the average figure for the previous *thirty* years, 1950–80 (8.6 per cent), then the Reagan figure is obviously well below the average. Of course, when only current dollar costs are quoted, the rate of inflation and the growth of real national income over those three decades makes the Reagan figures look enormous. And if, for purposes of making a political point either for or against Carter or Reagan, one chooses the 4.7 per cent figure for 1979 as a base, the proportional increase in the Reagan years over the Carter years does also look substantial. But not, as this argument has hoped to show, if you take the longer-term view of the level of US defence expenditure in the postwar patch of history to date. And to stress against an earlier point of some political significance, since both real and nominal national income per capita was very much lower in the earlier decades of the postwar period than in the Reagan years, the level of real sacrifice imposed then by high defence costs was much more substantial. Indeed, in an odd way the Reagan economic policies seem to have actually managed to postpone the impact of his Administration's defence spending to some indefinite future date, after the President's term of office. For the growth in defence spending ran roughly parallel to the balance of payments deficit, and that in turn was financed largely by the inflow of foreign capital into the United States, an inflow induced partly by the higher interest rates required by the budget deficit. So if one is seeking to locate the group which finally 'picked up the tab' for the Reagan defence budgets, one might say it was initially those who paid the higher interest rates (business men and home-buyers, though even they could largely offset it against tax); but foreigners at the time lent a good deal of the money, so that there was an increase in national debt to be serviced from future national income. In other words, the sacrifices were largely deferred, and thus very little immediate pain was inflicted on the electorate in either the way of taxes or of inflation. This might be regarded either as a neat economic trick or a dereliction of duty according to one's point of view, but undoubtedly it conduced for quite a while to the continued political popularity of the Administration, and especially of the President personally.

Soviet defence expenditure has normally been much higher as a proportion of GNP than American: the usual estimate is 12–14 per cent, but some analysts put it as high as 17–20 per cent. And that is of a much lower real national income per capita: less than 60 per cent of the US level on average over the four decades. So the degree of real sacrifice imposed by the arms race on Soviet society has been and continues to be much greater: probably about three times the American level. There is also, of course, the personal cost to the young Soviet male citizen of the years he compulsorily spends as a low-paid soldier-conscript, a cost difficult to quantify but offset by some 'socialization' advantages to the Soviet system and perhaps to the individual.

One of the other points that must be borne in mind when contemplating the relation between defence expenditure and the actual defence establishment is that one must discount not only for the ordinary inflation rate of the period under review but also for a specific 'defence goods inflation rate' (perhaps partly due to 'goldplating') which seems to ensure that each successive generation of any given weapons-system will cost at least four times the previous generation of that kind of weapons-system. As they say round the Pentagon, 'a billion dollars is not what it used to be'. It will buy barely half an aircraft carrier, for instance.

Resentments generated by the more visible and bizarre examples of the special defence-costs inflation rate, along with alarm at the ballooning-out of the deficits, were what helped get the Gramm–Rudman–Hollings deficit-reduction Act passed by Congress, with the President's approval, in December 1985. The effect of the measure (despite the constitutional doubts about some of its provisions) along with the general weakening of the defence consensus was to revise sharply downwards previous expectations of the 'staying power' of the Reagan defence commitment, especially in view of the Democratic majority in both houses after the 1986 mid-term elections. In the Budget request sent to Congress in January 1987, the defence funds asked for 1988 were $303 billion, quite a fall from the $377 billion originally postulated for 1988. And even that was further reduced by Congress, the House cutting it to $295 billion. Defence budgets fell steadily in real terms during the final Reagan years (after 1985), and it appeared probable that the level as his successor inherited office would fall below 5.9 per cent of GNP. Though that figure would by most analysts be seen as quite adequate to cover all existing US commitments (plus an allocation for SDI research), if one contrasts it with the 1981 figure of 5.5 per cent – which still reflected the final Carter decisions – it meant that the alleged 'great leap upward' of Reagan defence budgets had ended in the unspectacular figure of 0.4 of one per cent of GNP.

To sum up, though the Reagan Administration did undoubtedly effect a build-up of American military muscle *vis-à-vis* the Soviet Union, and the diplomatic effects of the *declaration* of projected increases were initially (for good and ill) quite dramatic, the effort was not as unparalleled as was sometimes alleged, or as long-sustained as was originally expected. By 1986 right-wing analysts were arguing that the Reagan defence 'boom' had been followed by a defence 'bust'. Moreover, if one contrasts the Reagan years not with the 'Vietnam syndrome' years, but with averages for the postwar decades as a whole, even the initially postulated budgets do not seem all that phenomenal. When he came to office, the *image* of American military power was looking rather inadequate, at least in some US eyes (though not necessarily in the eyes of adversaries or allies), mostly on account of concepts like that of the 'window of vulnerability', which had been given credibility largely through the efforts of Reagan supporters. The President was able to undo that always somewhat misleading impression by the strength of his declaratory policy and by gestures like appointing the Scowcroft Committee, which in due course declared the 'window of vulnerability' closed. So undoubtedly during the Reagan period a great deal of burnishing was devoted to the *image* of American military power. The reality (according to the judgement of relatively non-partisan expert opinion) of the vast American armoury had never been in all that much need of major repair-work, other than the modernization of missile forces to match what the Soviet Union had done during the 1970s. That was achieved in the early Reagan years, with the rapid increase in the rate of procurement of both strategic and theatre nuclear warheads. The changed political climate of the two final Reagan years, after Republican loss of control of the Senate in November 1986 and loss of the original political consensus behind the ambitious initial arms budgets, made the last phase of his Presidency uncongenial for new efforts on offensive missile systems and such, as also did the changed diplomatic climate on arms control.

Along with 'Irancontragate', that changed climate on arms control was perhaps the largest single surprise of the Reagan period in foreign policy. Until the summit meeting at Reykjavik in October 1986, most of those who took an informed interest in the details of arms-control negotiations between the superpowers had been pessimistic about the probability of any substantial agreement in this field between Moscow and Washington during the Reagan years. Strobe Talbot's book *Deadly Gambits* had provided a detailed and highly convincing view of a political bargaining-process in Washington from which it seemed unlikely that any hopeful initiative would emerge. And the Russians seemed to have 'quit the game' even in the public opinion contest, with their ostentatious walk-out from the negotiations in 1983 during their vain effort to prevent the European missile deployment.

So not much was originally expected of Reykjavik: it was billed in the US as a 'pre-summit' rather than the authentic article. Yet the combination, apparently, of considerable diplomatic gamesmanship on the part of the Russians with some unwary 'talking-off-the-cuff' on the part of Mr Reagan transformed it into an occasion from which wildly radical proposals, by previous standards of serious negotiations, seemed suddenly to emerge on both sides. Even after the 'playing to the gallery' elements in the two positions had been eliminated, what was left, and seemed to be genuinely on the table, implied a striking reversal of the strategic doctrines and expectations of the past few decades. Sufficiently, in fact, greatly to disconcert both the NATO 'top brass', and the political leaders of West European countries in the alliance. Neither group had been consulted in advance.

Perhaps it is only when such usual 'veto groups' are left out of the preliminary negotiations that proposals as far-reaching as those of Reykjavik can be aired. The most important possibilities contemplated were: first, a cut in strategic nuclear warheads to 6000 on each side; secondly, a cut in delivery vehicles of all kinds to about 1600 on each side; and thirdly, elimination of intermediate range missiles; in the final revisions this was extended to a 'global double zero' in Asia as well as Europe.

Even more unexpected notions were put forward as possibilities for the longer-term future. The American intention had apparently been to propose the elimination of *strategic ballistic* missiles within ten years, but by a slip of the tongue President Reagan seems to have said 'strategic forces', which would of course imply eliminating other systems (like cruise) as well, thus greatly reducing the effectiveness of US strike capacity. Moreover, since the original rationale of SDI was to make nuclear weapons 'impotent and obsolete', there had to be US assent, at least as a distant aspiration, to Mr Gorbachev's proposal for the elimination of nuclear weapons in general.

Such ideas, if taken seriously, would require remaking the entire strategic basis on which NATO has operated for forty years, which postulates not only nuclear weapons, but *first use* of nuclear weapons, as a balance against the still real (though often exaggerated) Soviet advantage in conventional forces. So it was not surprising that the NATO establishment, both political and military, was more than a little ruffled by the reports out of Reykjavik. Moreover, the whole package was initially presented as non-negotiable because of the two sides' conflicting positions on SDI. The President was thus originally cast by many Western commentators in the role of the decision-maker who had allowed his obsession with an allegedly unworkable system to stand in the way of the most promising arms control 'package deal' of the nuclear age.

Elimination or very severe reduction in numbers of ballistic missiles (especially land-based fixed-site mirved ballistic missiles), if it can be done in an even-handed and verifiable fashion, has enormous advantages as a measure of arms control. Ballistic missiles are the most dangerous 'hairtrigger' element in the present strategic balance, because of their 'prompt' delivery. Other modes of delivery, 'air-breathing systems' as they are called (cruise missiles and aircraft and the rest), may allow at least some hours for reflection or negotiation and can in some cases be recalled or aborted. It is not likely for the foreseeable future that NATO could seriously agree to the elimination of nuclear weapons in general (not even if an SDI system were effectively in operation, and whatever the president's personal aspirations) because of the very reasonable European fears of what Soviet conventional forces might be tempted to do, in a major crisis, in the absence of the nuclear balance. But both sides could see a gain for stability in dispensing with the 'hairtrigger' factor intrinsic to ballistic weapons, as against the other modes of delivery. And if there were, in conjunction with that, a build-up in Western Europe of 'smart' weapons with conventional warheads to check the formidable Soviet tank armies in Eastern Europe, it might become feasible for NATO to move, in due course, towards a 'no first use' doctrine concerning nuclear weapons. So the talks at Reykjavik had to be regarded as having offered a first fleeting glimpse of a feasible pathway by which the central balance powers could make their way towards a less dangerous *modus vivendi*. But being suddenly faced with the possible need to function during a positive earthquake of strategic and consequent diplomatic change left a lot of NATO policy-makers quite bemused, and more alarmed than hopeful, immediately after the summit meeting.

From one angle, the Soviet case against SDI had been enhanced by giving that concept the status of (at first glance) the only obstacle to an apparently desirable arms-control agreement. But the chief surprise was that the superpowers had suddenly appeared to come so close together, rather than that they had failed to clinch the deal. For hardly anyone, at least in the military and foreign policy establishments, had expected any change at all, let alone so dramatic a prospect as that which emerged. A day or two before the summit, they were forecasting that it would produce only benevolent platitudes, 'photo-opportunities' and, at best, a very slight 'impulse' to the log-jam in arms control. Whereas after the meeting and during the final two years of the Reagan presidency, it appeared even to well-informed observers that the logs were moving with unexpected speed down the river and would almost certainly by his final months or soon afterwards reach some destination: whether desirable or undesirable remained a matter of argument within the NATO military and diplomatic establishments.

The most paradoxical element in the whole episode was its longer-term effect on attitudes towards SDI. The apparent demonstration that Soviet decision-makers could be contemplating the phasing-out, even as a distant vision, of the ballistic missiles to which they have over the past thirty years been devoting vast resources they could ill spare from other uses was clearly a striking tribute to the strength of the SDI concept as a negotiating lever. Negotiating lever rather than bargaining-chip, though the distinction between the two concepts seemed not to be appreciated by many of the commentators after Reykjavik. A bargaining-chip is by definition something you are prepared to trade away: to abandon it as you use it. A negotiating lever is more like a tyre-lever: you do not abandon it, at least until you get the vehicle where you want it to go. Reykjavik represented only a mile or two along that road, though in an unexpectedly promising direction.

In terms of the underlying diplomacy of Reykjavik, Mr Gorbachev initially appeared in a 'no lose' situation. He could be 99 per cent certain (when offering his radical arms control package on condition of restriction of SDI development) that President Reagan would refuse, his commitment to the SDI concept being so firm. Mr Gorbachev could also be certain that refusal would irk the Europeans, who had little or no faith in SDI, and thus produce some further fraying of NATO relationships. He could additionally hope for some influence on Congressional attitudes in Washington, in the sense that willingness to fund SDI might be still further diminished if it appeared the major obstacle to an apparently attractive arms-control bargain. And there might be a prospect that the choice of Republican and Democratic candidates (one of whom would be his 'opposite number' relatively soon in Washington) would be influenced in the direction of those sceptical or ambivalent about SDI. Thus the occasion offered an almost irresistible chance of some Soviet diplomatic gamesmanship. In the event, however, the outcome was rather different. Those who had argued that SDI was strictly just a fantasy out of 'Star Trek' had to explain why, in that case, the Russians (who had done a great deal of strategic defence research themselves, and who might be expected to know the technologies a lot better than most Westerners) were making such assiduous efforts towards eliminating it. If Soviet technological experience had indicated such schemes were on balance not cost-effective, surely the logical course of Soviet action was to encourage them by whatever means came to hand, since while the Americans were pouring some of their resources into a bottomless scientific pit of useless effort, there would be so much the less for them to spend on solidly practical strategic hardware, like long-range offensive cruise missiles with 'Stealth' technology, nuclear submarines, aircraft carriers and so on.

The Russians and those critical or sceptical of SDI tended to reply that though SDI would be ineffective in a purely defensive role, such as Mr Reagan had propounded, it might nevertheless become effective enough to absorb a 'ragged' Soviet retaliatory strike after an American pre-emptive strike. In a curious way, however, that reasoning, propounded by the enemies of SDI, provided it with an unexpected new justification in the context of the arms-control proposals at Reykjavik. For if ballistic missiles were about to be reduced to much lower numbers, which seemed probable, or even *nominally* eliminated within ten years or by 2000, which seemed just possible (though very unlikely), each of the superpowers would in consequence become far more vulnerable to 'cheating' on the part of the other. Even a hundred ballistic missiles with nuclear warheads, secreted away and suddenly produced in the context of crisis, could provide a decisive edge of advantage, both diplomatically and strategically, to the side that had cheated.

Unless, of course, either or both had in existence an SDI able to cope with such small numbers. Moreover, the minor nuclear powers – Britain, France, China, probably Israel, possibly in time South Africa or India, or Pakistan, or Argentina – could all conceivably achieve a considerable level of ballistic nuclear capacity: some already have both missile and nuclear technology. Not all of them will necessarily be persuaded to go along with a superpower ban, and their total warhead numbers could within the time-frame contemplated be rising towards 2000 or so. (Though at present about 97 per cent of all nuclear weapons are in the hands of the two superpowers, that figure will change substantially if the present proposals go into effect.) Thus SDI systems would have a potential function also as the most feasible mode of insuring against 'third parties' for both superpowers, assuming that both continue the research on which each is at present engaged. In effect, therefore, the prospect of a successful arms-control curb on (or the near-elimination of) the most dangerous mode of delivery of offensive nuclear weapons (mirved land-based fixed-site ballistic missiles) could paradoxically be held to improve the case for SDI, rather than undermine it.

If there is ever to be a transition from deterrence based (as now) on offensive-strike capacity ('deterrence by punishment') to deterrence based on defensive capacity ('deterrence by denial'), it will undoubtedly have to move through some system of 'trade-offs' between offensive and defensive weaponry. That will be a very dangerous process; yet in the period after Reykjavik, and more especially the period after 'Irancontragate', that possible path towards arms control seemed suddenly and surprisingly to be opening up. For Mr Reagan had an extra incentive to forward some treaties which might stand to his name in future world history. And Mr Gorbachev had reason to want negotiations that would reduce the probability, in the early Bush years, of a vigorous push towards early deployment of some rudimentary version of SDI. He had also to reckon that unless something were achieved in the Reagan period, he might conceivably have to wait two or three years while the then–unknown new incumbent turned his mind to other matters, by which time unpredictable possibilities might emerge from SDI. Thus, as the Presidential election came in sight, there appeared also the distant chance of more arms-control treaties than any year since 1972.

In retrospect, the Reagan policies in the whole area of arms and arms control may be seen as a particularly striking instance of a reversal of signals by the administration. That is to say, the initial signal was 'more arms, less arms control (if any)'. But the final outcome, as the election year went on, encouraged expectations of rather more notable change in future arms-control prospects than in the future US strategic establishment. The 'double zero' agreement on intermediate-range nuclear forces (long-range or LRINF and shorter-range or SRINF) appeared to have developed a tendency to promote a 'triple zero' future development, with the possible elimination also of short-range systems (SNF) under 500 kilometres in Europe. A little-publicized evolution in crisis-management techniques, the setting-up of nuclear-risk reduction centres in Washington and Moscow (manned on a 24-hour basis, with 'hotline', by diplomatic and military personnel in each capital) had been agreed, and also some important 'confidence-building measures' which had emerged from the Stockholm meeting, the descendant of the Helsinki meeting which Mr Reagan used to attack assiduously as a symbol of a despised détente. That word was still avoided by Reagan policy-makers, but it had become difficult to see what other term was applicable in 1987–8 to Western (including US) relations with Moscow.

More importantly still, the consequences in Europe of a decision to eliminate the intermediate-range nuclear weapons were already profound, diplomatically and politically as well as strategically, and likely to become more so. The original 1979 decision for their deployment (the 'two-tracks' NATO decision pushed mostly by Helmut Schmidt as Chancellor of West Germany) had always had much more a diplomatic and political rationale than a military one. In a situation in which the Soviet Union had been upgrading its intermediate-range missiles (which can reach practically all European targets, but not American ones), the Europeans, especially the West Germans, felt an extra vulnerability and thus a need for reassurance that the superpowers would not reach a tacit understanding to fight out any nuclear conflict only on West and East European soil, with Soviet and American territory silently exempted. The intermediate-range forces ruled out that possibility, since Soviet (though not American) targets were within their range. That very fact gave Soviet decision-makers an extra reason, of course, for wanting their elimination. Thus, though Mr Gorbachev at Reykjavik originally tied intermediate as well as strategic missiles to the SDI issue, he came off that position in March 1987, and the proposal for the elimination of that category of weapons was able to go rapidly ahead.

The effect was to restore the probable strategic 'scenario' in the event of central-balance war to what it had been in the late 1960s: a conventional battle rapidly (perhaps within three days) turning into a nuclear one, mostly on German soil, with an almost unimaginable level of destruction throughout Central Europe. So when it became clear that the intermediate-range weapons were likely to be phased out, the case was rapidly strengthened, at least in German eyes, for the elimination also of the US short-range battlefield and tactical weapons (missiles, artillery-shells, land-mines and dual-capable aircraft). The nature of the contemporary balance of power makes it almost inevitable that any future European battlefield will be on German soil: that is the ultimate penalty for the Hitler years. Germans both east and west of the divide thus had the strongest conceivable reasons for preferring a conventional to a tactical-nuclear defensive strategy for NATO, but only the evolution of 'smart' weapons (especially anti-tank guided missiles with conventional warheads) during the past decade had made that option look feasible.

The case *against* phasing out battlefield nuclear weapons had always been the proposition that to do so would make the continent 'safe for conventional war'. And the Europeans, especially the Germans, could remember what the scale of destruction of conventional war was almost half a century ago. So they had for thirty years preferred the dangers of the tactical nuclear balance to the dangers of making conventional war even slightly more probable. But once the nuclear relationship was seen to be changing radically for reasons outside their control, they became obliged to rethink their overall strategy, and even their choice of major strategic partnerships, in the general design of European defence. One of the possible directions of change proposed by unofficial but very well informed German opinion was that, in effect, the SALT I principle of 'putting the missiles out to sea' should be revived: that the short-range nuclear weapons in Europe be replaced by sea-launched cruise missiles (Tomahawk) installed on US ships 'home-ported' in Europe and under the command of the NATO Commander-in-Chief, who will presumably continue to be an American, at least for the foreseeable future.

The arms-control negotiations on conventional manpower levels in central Europe (MBFR) which had been in effect marking time for fifteen years with practically no progress whatever, also seemed to be impelled in new directions. One basic difficulty was that the Western powers had during those years been conscious that their conventional forces needed to be built up rather than cut, if Europe was ever to escape from 'first use' reliance on tactical nuclear weapons, and Soviet policy-makers had no incentive for unilateral concessions. But in the new arms-control climate, there appeared possible 'trade-offs' that would reduce both sides' fear of surprise attack: for instance, a ceiling on Soviet tank-armies for a pull-back or elimination of Western forward-based systems. A new basis for talks, to replace MBFR, covering the whole NATO–Warsaw Pact balance and considering weaponry as well as manpower numbers, had been agreed by the end of 1988. The notion of the 'denuclearization' or 'conventionalization' of European defence, at least in terms of battlefield and tactical systems, had come under debate in the discourse of strategic analysts from 1987.

All these changes operated to enhance the importance of the two long-range European nuclear forces, those of France and Britain. Together they could undoubtedly deploy, within the time scale being contemplated in the arms-talks, well over a thousand warheads, mostly on sophisticated delivery-systems launched from relatively invulnerable platforms (nuclear-powered submarines protected by strong ASW capabilities). While an American strategic force ten times the size remained firmly 'coupled' to European defence, Europe's own two nuclear forces had not been of much true strategic importance: Mr Gorbachev thus could agree at Reykjavik that they be left out of the equations. But if the superpowers' forces actually were as drastically cut as had been envisaged, there would probably tend to occur an evolution from 'extended deterrence' towards some new system, with or without SDI. And given the implications of the changes being contemplated, the two European nuclear forces might well seem at least as convincing as the American one for inhibiting any major challenge in Europe; especially as the Bush policy-makers and Congress appear at least as likely as those of the late Reagan years to regard the United States as over-extended, militarily and economically.

The urges to cut US defence budgets and bring at least some of the American troops in Europe back home are clearly very strong in both élite and grass-roots opinion, and not likely to diminish.

West Europeans were by the Reagan years not only more numerous than Americans (320 million), they were also getting to be as rich or nearly so. When the original expectation was established in the early 1950s that the US would normally spend a higher percentage of GNP on defence than the Europeans, the rationale was that a rich country could afford to devote a lot more of its resources to military goods and services than a group of poorer ones. But the Europeans could hardly rely on that argument in the late 1980s, and their sense of common identity, common interests and potentially a common political will had grown quite substantially in NATO's four decades. Indeed, they had already been pushing arms-control proposals of particular European interest quite effectively themselves, in the Stockholm 'confidence-building measures' (agreed surveillance of Soviet and Western military exercises) and a set of negotiations to control chemical weapons (elimination of gas warfare capabilities).

With these possibilities moving towards fruition by January 1989, the arms-control community had to concede (though with ill-disguised reluctance as far as its Utopian left wing was concerned) that, contrary to prophecy, the late Reagan years had turned out to be quite a vintage period for arms control. But almost everything which engendered that surprising outcome was at odds with the prescriptions of even the less Utopian strategists of arms control. In the words of an eminent expert, it was ironical 'that a president who is untutored in Western arms control theory – heading an administration that is largely unsympathetic to arms control and holds outdated assumptions about Soviet doctrine – should have engendered a situation so favourable to achieving major reductions in nuclear weapons'. Spokespersons for the arms-control movement had originally argued that INF deployment would end Soviet interest in arms control, but in fact, the European demonstration after 1983 that their governments would deploy, regardless, brought the Russians back into the talks. Many friends of arms control then argued that the breaching of the SALT II limits would end all prospect of its realization, but in fact, proposals came faster in the year or so after that happened than before it. They likewise argued that the 'Star Wars' idea would be the kiss of death for arms control, but possibly it proved the most effective negotiating lever that the West ever invented in that field of diplomacy, even if it was rather a strategic confidence trick.

However, even if they had to do so through gritted teeth, the friends of arms control could nevertheless endorse the end result with genuine enthusiasm. Many of Mr Reagan's original supporters on the far right, and some independent strategic analysts of high standing, were not able to echo their views. The most notable of the latter group was General Bernard Rogers, the former NATO Commander-in-Chief, who had been widely regarded in Europe as the most successful holder of that office since Eisenhower. He bluntly called the arms proposals 'madness' and attributed a political motive to them.[20] The French Defence Minister talked of a 'nuclear Munich', and the British government, while approving, spoke of 'cosmic changes' being imposed on NATO strategy.

Those reactions were not all alarmist: they reflected the sense, in some very well-informed quarters, that the whole foundation of a Western strategic position that had proved stable for almost forty years (and that has had many advantages despite its costs and dangers) had suddenly crumbled away like a sandcastle when the tide comes in; and that, what was worse, this surprise had been engineered in the time of a President whom they had originally seen as the best possible bulwark against anything of the sort.

Part of the reason for the dramatic reversal of signals in this field was perhaps that a President with too short an attention-span to master his brief on so complex an issue as the long-range strategic implications of arms-control proposals, had not been able to match the adroitness and flexibility of Mr Gorbachev, who seemed able to make more radical changes in the Soviet position than any of his predecessors. That showed up with particular clarity on questions like inspection and verification, on which American and Soviet negotiators appear to have almost changed places. Those who ingeniously took over the left-wing German '*null lösung*' slogan and turned it into the 'zero option' which went into the 1981 American proposals were presumably trying the technique of 'making the Russians an offer they are bound to refuse'. It was that offer which Mr Gorbachev still more ingeniously accepted in 1986, to the discomfort of some, at least, of those who had used it as a negotiating ploy. That may seem paradoxical enough, but still more so was the probability that the combined effects of these two pieces of disingenuous arms-control gamesmanship would actually be to send the whole arms-control enterprise a long way towards some actual arms reductions.

In the weeks between the US election and President Bush's inauguration, especially just after Mr Gorbachev's truly remarkable UN speech of 7 December 1988, that prospect appeared almost implausibly hopeful. The proposals for unilateral Soviet reductions seemed initially so stunning in their magnitude that Western commentators were reduced to assuming that there must be some traps in the 'small print'. A great many strategic and political assumptions had suddenly to be revised. The subsequent working out of new Western positions will be considered in the final chapter.

5. Terrorists and Contention: The Middle East

The most damaging débâcle of the Reagan period, the Iran imbroglio, was particularly rich in paradox, including the fact that it was not a true international crisis at all, only a foreign-policy crisis. The Administration was no more in confrontation with the regime in Nicaragua than it had been ever since Mr Reagan came to office, and in a kind of accidental (on the US side) collusion with that in Iran. Ayatollah Khomeini had reason enough for sardonic laughter if he followed all the long-term repercussions from the seizure of American hostages by Iran's friends. The true confrontation was, like so much else in the Reagan policies, between words and deeds, between the declaratory and the operational signals of the Administration. It thus represented the most visible exemplification of a technique which (as this study has hoped to show) had been in operation for the whole history of the Administration and had perhaps produced some earlier successes. 'Irancontragate' was the occasion on which it went catastrophically and all too openly wrong, reducing the operations of the National Security Council to the level of a television 'cloak and dagger' series.

The major effects were domestic, rather than international. It did of course damage the standing of the Administration with America's allies, and especially with the quasi-allies of the Arab world. But by late 1986, when the story began to break publicly, the Administration's diplomatic esteem in those circles was so low anyway that any further reduction was not of much consequence. Possibly it also affected the President's standing as a negotiator *vis-à-vis* Mr Gorbachev, but (on the evidence of the arms-control proposals) that was interpreted in Moscow as a reason for pressing on rather than for drawing back. There were some tactical advantages to be found from a Soviet point of view, and little or nothing to lose, by negotiation with an American President who had only two more years of office as a 'lame duck', with no majority in either the House or the Senate. The logical effect in Moscow obviously also included stepped-up and revised calculations about the President's possible successors and how to influence them. Among American allies, the probability that US arms were continuing to go to the *Contras* in defiance of Congress had been already widely taken for granted, even by conservative commentators. Foreign-policy establishments already tended to see the efforts to overturn that government as ill-considered and counter-productive, and public opinion to see such efforts as immoral, so there was no great scope for disillusionment left. Evidence that US arms had gone to the Iranians as well did certainly evoke more surprise but with initially commendatory overtones, since the argument presented as a mere cover-story in Washington was one that European analysis had for some time been more serious in propounding. The reasoning went thus: geopolitics and oil dictate that the government in Iran must remain important to the West, and on the oil side even more important to Europeans and Japanese than to Americans. The Ayatollah will probably not live for ever and a subdued conflict over the succession is visibly under way in Teheran. If Washington can begin to come to terms with the less intransigent groups among possible successors, it may pay off in the longer term for the West as a whole. And if that requires some arms deliveries (though not enough, of course, to enable Iran to win the war) it is a reasonable gamble to take. The primary aim must still be the exclusion of Soviet power from the Persian Gulf, and to that end NATO must promote as far as possible a stable Iran with a pragmatic government (hopefully) and an equable relationship with the West. The present fundamentalist revolutionary leadership may be passing: we must try to be in on the ground floor with the next lot or the Russians will beat us to it.

This kind of standard geopolitical reasoning was not necessarily offset by the discovery that a US deal over the delivery of hostages had also been included in the package. Several European governments (especially France and Italy) had earlier been on the receiving end of pious Washington lectures about the reprehensible idiocy of dealing with, or making any concessions to, terrorists. So there was some understandable *schadenfreude* in the reaction of those concerned to the public revelation that some of President

Reagan's closest aides had surreptitiously gone into the business of buying-out hostages by the delivery of US arms to the Ayatollah's government. For the Europeans, it was rather like gleefully discovering a TV evangelist drunk in a seedy brothel.

In the earlier years of the Administration, the focus of the US anti-terrorism drive had been against Colonel Gaddafi, presented by Washington as playing the primary role in supporting, inspiring, financing and propounding terrorism as a political and diplomatic instrument. That was always rather overrating his real importance, but the flamboyance of Gaddafi's personality and attitudes made him a natural target or whipping-boy, a proxy for governments more crucial but more discreet or less vulnerable, like Syria and Iran.

Given the circumstances in which Mr Reagan had come to office, it was probably inevitable that the terrorism issue would have to be played up, much more than had been done in the pre-1979 formulation of US Middle Eastern policy. The long anguish of the hostages in Teheran had dominated almost the whole period of the first Reagan election campaign and had settled the fate of his predecessor, Jimmy Carter. Preoccupation with the notion of state terrorism as a new and sinister technique by which 'rogue governments' like those in Libya or Iran or Syria could pursue diplomatic or political ends through the instrumentality of individual fanatics willing to die themselves (and very willing to kill or take hostage any American convenient to their hands), was a central topic of neo-conservative analysis. So the newly-elected President Reagan pledged in his first Inaugural Address 'swift and resolute' action against terrorists.

Unfortunately, as both official and non-official analysts have pointed out, announcing a preoccupation at the highest political level with terrorism means conceding the primary objective of the terrorists. They live on the oxygen of publicity, as Mrs Thatcher put it. Engineering a situation in which the welfare of some group of hostages becomes the top item on a President's agenda – whether the President is Jimmy Carter or Ronald Reagan – was in itself a triumph achieved, justifying their *raison d'être* and increasing their basic usefulness to the governments or political movements they served.

The logical way to defeat a strategy based on hostage-taking is not only 'no deals' but no publicity either. In a pluralistic society with highly independent media, like the US, that is unfortunately impossible, but various points about the Reagan diplomatic style made his administration even more tempting as a target than most. If you deal largely in images and 'photo-opportunities' as a foreign-policy technique, few things provide more touching images or better photo-opportunities than grateful released hostages and happily weeping wives shaking hands with the President. On the other hand, if you present international politics as a system of moral simplicities, you must expect the electorate in its turn to make simple moral judgements on your own policies. Most of the issues of international politics are too complex and obscure, and develop over too long a period, for the man-in-the-street to take much note of differences between the original words and the eventual deeds of his political leaders. But that is not the case with hostage-taking. The analogy with domestic kidnapping, and the obvious probability that paying off kidnappers will encourage more people to go into that business and so increase the general danger, is not likely to escape public notice. Moreover, there had been all those statements of American principle, and all those well-publicized chidings of allegedly more weak-kneed allies, like the Italians over the *Achille Lauro* episode and everyone but the British over reluctance to be implicated in the strike against Colonel Gaddafi. All that gave the issue a salience that could only prove dangerous to the President.

The first stone in the eventual avalanche of evidence that American operational policies were not matching the tough-mindedness of the declaratory ones came over the Daniloff affair: the swapping (obvious though denied) of a Soviet intelligence agent arrested in New York for a hostage journalist picked up in reprisal by the KGB in Moscow. But as far as the general purposes of American foreign policy were concerned, it was, of course, in Middle East relationships that the terrorist issue did its most notable damage. That damage began as early as 1981 with the distortion, subtle but pervasive, through which long-term interests tended to be crowded out of the attention of both policy-makers and the public by short-term dramas. Those dramas (and the effort at 'happy endings') provided the sort of context in which Lt.-Col. Oliver North and 'Project Democracy' could endow important areas of US foreign policy with a 'gung-ho' crusading quality that made for very lively media stories, and eventually for political and diplomatic embarrassments. In time, those embarrassments came home to Washington, of course, but in the pre-disclosure period they were mostly a problem for America's remaining friends in the Arab world, like Egypt, and for Western allies like Italy or Britain.

Before the Iran imbroglio became public, the change of emphasis had been visible in the focus, from the earliest months of the Reagan first term, on Colonel Gaddafi and the hatching of projects to cut him down to size. By June 1981 reports were circulating in Washington that the National Security Council had taken over the problem: in view of the subsequent saga of Colonel North's activities, those reports must be regarded as initial signals of the later storm. But nothing much came of them during the first Reagan term, aside from the skirmish over the Gulf of Sidra in August 1981. Later that year publicity or 'disinformation' was generated concerning possible Libyan 'hit teams' in America, inferentially looking for targets which might include the President himself. If that was intended as a declaratory signal to warn Gaddafi of possible US equivalent operations in future, it also seemed to go underground for several years.

There were various reasons for a relatively slow hardening of determination to act. The decline in oil prices, and Gaddafi's own decision to cut production, were reducing the funds at Libya's disposal from a high point of about $22 billion to about $5 billion by early 1986, and some expert opinion was of the view that this in itself would considerably cramp his ability to make trouble. Libya's capacity to export oil could, of course, have been crippled, or even ended for a time, by mining the harbours at which the tankers were loaded, or by striking directly at jetties or the oil installations themselves. But that would have endangered the lives of the many non-Libyans who worked the oil fields. As late as 1986 there were estimated to still be about 1500 Americans, 5000 British and many Italian, West German, Turkish and other foreigners working in Libyan cities or oil installations. They had to be regarded not only as potential victims but as potential hostages, even though there was no signal of the likelihood of their being seized. The respective governments of these expatriate workers had no way of enforcing their departure, and since they mostly held very well-paid jobs no government exhortations were likely to induce them to quit of their own accord. Moreover, even if they had made a mass exit, Western long-term interests would not necessarily have been served, since their replacements would probably have come from Warsaw Pact countries, and the dangers of Libya being edged more fully into the Soviet sphere of influence (perhaps in the time of Gaddafi's successor) would have been increased. America's European allies, especially Italy and West Germany, maintained profitable trade relations with Libya and were not prepared to impose sanctions. Even though European streets and airports had been the scene of many terrorist attacks and of the hunting-down of Libyan dissidents by the 'hit squads' of the Gaddafi regime, the affected governments, even in Britain, were on the whole inclined to see terrorism as something which had to be contained by defensive operations, and they were sceptical of its being 'cured' by a strike at one of its sources. The decision-makers involved had some reason, on experience, for believing that the effort at a cure might prove worse than the disease. They had lived longer with various terrorist groups – IRA, ETA, Red Brigades and the rest – and were more conscious than Washington seemed to be that the problem had no rapid solutions.

Early in the second term three terrorist incidents in close succession brought matters to the boil for the Reagan policy-makers. The first, the seizure of a TWA aircraft in June 1985 and the murder of an American passenger, Robert Stethem, was the work of Shiah radicals affiliated to the Lebanese militia, AMAL. Though most of the passengers were rescued after being held for some days at Beirut airport with (as was afterwards revealed) some Syrian and Iranian help, the fact that the perpetrators were allowed to escape and secure some of their objectives, brought heavy criticism of President Reagan, especially from neo-conservatives who had earlier been among his most ardent supporters. Norman Podhoretz, for instance, wrote that policy had been 'public bravado combined with a privately negotiated surrender' and went on to draw the moral for the Soviet Union:

> the United States, even under the fearsome Ronald Reagan is unwilling to use force even against an aggressor with the power to threaten only a few American lives.
>
> Why then should the Soviets or anyone else believe we will risk millions of American lives in response to a Soviet attack on Europe – or for that matter a threatened attack on the United States itself?[21]

The incident, or such criticisms, reinvigorated the discussions at the National Security Council of measures that might prove feasible against Gaddafi, including the notion of covertly fomenting a *coup* against him, or a direct military attack by Egyptian forces with covert US aid. (The Egyptians refused to play ball.) The hijacking of the *Achille Lauro* cruise-ship in October, with the cold-blooded murder of a crippled Jewish-American, and the airport attacks at Rome and Vienna in December 1985 contributed to the hardening resolution in Washington. In March 1986 the decision for 'Operation Prairie Fire', a deliberate challenge in the Gulf of Sidra, was agreed by the President and put into the hands of Admiral Frank Kelso, the Commander of the US Sixth Fleet in the Mediterranean. Three US aircraft-carriers – the *America*, the *Saratoga* and the *Coral Sea* – along with Hawkeye and Prowler aircraft, Los Angeles-class submarines, and HARM and Harpoon missiles were used on the American side: Soviet SA–5s on the Libyan side. In the subsequent battle of advanced technologies, the US equipment appeared to come out a clear winner. In case any Soviet personnel should find themselves in danger, Washington explicitly told Moscow in advance what was planned, so that the Russians could get their people away, if they chose, and light up their communication ship at Surt so that it should not be targeted. Presumably the Russians told the Libyans what was coming, but that, of course, merely underlined their inability to do anything about it.

Taking issue with Libya specifically over its stance on the Gulf of Sidra had considerable political and diplomatic advantages from the point of view of Washington policy-makers. The US government, and most other members of the society of states, regarded the Gulf as just a stretch of the Mediterranean: international waters and therefore fully subject to 'innocent passage', even by warships. Colonel Gaddafi, on the other hand, had since 1973 defined the Gulf as 'internal waters' (not merely 'territorial waters') for Libya, on the basis of a line drawn between two points on the Libyan coastline. 'Internal waters' are subject to the sovereignty of the country which surrounds them, and there are some large almost-enclosed gulfs, like Hudson's Bay in Canada, which have long been conceded by international law and custom to have that historical character. But the Gulf of Sidra was not one of them, and in the narrow waters of the Mediterranean it was to the general interest of the maritime powers that any such encroachments in the name of sovereignty be resisted on principle. It was also, of course, to the national interest of the United States as the dominant naval power in the Mediterranean that its fleet be able to exercise unimpeded, and that there should not be the faintest shadow of appearance of yielding to any kind of illegitimate harassment.

No real effort was made, however, to disguise the fact that the operation was a warning-signal about Libyan-inspired terrorism rather than about maritime navigation rights. Colonel Gaddafi apparently chose to reply with a new terrorist attack: a bomb in a discothèque in Berlin at a time when it was sure to be full of young American soldiers. One of them and a Turkish woman were killed: more than two hundred people were injured.

Thus, by mid-April 1986 matters had come to the point of drawn battle between the Reagan administration and Colonel Gaddafi, standing in effect as a symbol and a proxy for other terrorists. There was no assurance that those in Iran or Syria or Lebanon or Yemen who made most of the decisions that sent the terrorists on their way with bombs and other instruments of violent death would 'get the message', though that clearly was the hope in Washington, and President Reagan said almost as much a week or so later. Considered as a proxy, or even as a whipping-boy for the others or a mode of sending a signal, Gaddafi was a prudent choice. He was more diplomatically isolated and more strategically vulnerable than any other of the governments sponsoring terrorism: Syria had a friendship treaty with the Soviet Union and Iran was much less readily accessible to Western air and sea power, as well as being surrounded by Arab governments in delicate states of political health and being of long-term importance *vis-à-vis* the Soviet Union.

In the period of Washington debate about the wisdom of anti-terrorist strikes, it had been widely reported that Shultz was strongly in favour of some such action, but that Weinberger and presumably his Pentagon constituency were not convinced that an open military operation was necessarily the most effective response. Not long before the action went ahead, however, Weinberger said in a speech in Boston that 'terror is now a state-practised activity, a method of waging war'[22] planned, organized and financed by governments, not a private enterprise activity of fanatic individuals and groups. That was an important point to assert, for the rationale given for the Libya strike in international law was Article 51 of the UN Charter, providing for the right of self-defence. A terrorist attack thus needed to be defined as the act of a particular government in order to make military reprisals against that government legitimate in terms of international conventions. The US air strikes appeared, however, to be related not to the provision in the UN Charter but rather to the nineteenth-century doctrine of 'self-help and reprisals', under which the US Marines had first been sent to attack pirates on 'the shores of Tripoli' in 1804.

Apparent but probably doubtful evidence for Libyan complicity in the Berlin night-club bomb was provided to allies, even though it meant the US revealing that its intelligence services had broken the Libyan diplomatic cypher and were listening-in on messages from the government in Tripoli to its embassies (which it calls 'people's bureaux') abroad. The Libyan bureau in East Berlin was reported to have claimed credit for its success in arranging the Berlin bombing. The US air-strike was finally given the 'go' signal on 13 April, after a week in which the US Ambassador to the UN, Vernon Walters, visited London, Paris, Madrid, Bonn and Rome to consult American allies and secure their co-operation if possible. He was successful only in London, where Margaret Thatcher agreed that F–111s from British bases should be used in the raid. France and Spain refused overflight permission, and most of the European policy-makers reportedly tried to talk Washington out of its decision, fearing that the raid would merely spur reprisal attacks against their own citizens. Ambassador Walters made no attempt to disguise his irritation at their recalcitrance and timidity when he talked to the press afterwards.[23]

Moscow, on the other hand, seemed to make very little effort to prevent the bombing, providing, indeed, what seemed very clear signals that it was not prepared to put any Soviet interest on the line to stop the Americans, though afterwards a scheduled meeting between Schultz and Shevardnadze was cancelled. Earlier, Arbatov had been allowed to go on the air speaking disrespectfully of Gaddafi.[24] Though the Soviet Union had sold Libya arms to the tune of about $15 billion and was estimated to have about 5000 military advisers in the country, relations between Moscow and Tripoli were very cool. Soviet policy-makers had reason to distrust Gaddafi's support for Islamic radicalism, which could be a potent source of domestic trouble in the Soviet Central Asian republics. A

Gaddafi visit to Moscow the previous October had been quite a disaster: it produced no friendship treaty and Gaddafi pointedly failed to attend the final reception in his own honour. The Soviet Union had refrained from showing much reaction to the earlier Gulf of Sidra attacks, and its general attitude in Third World crises for more than a decade (at least since the 1973 war) had shown no signs of a tendency to take risks even for more important friends than Gaddafi, for instance Syria. Soviet policy-makers could always console themselves for their inability to inhibit US action by reflecting that a 'Rambo' or 'trigger-happy cowboy' image of Reagan was bound to prove in their own long-term interests.

One of the reasons why the focus of the Reagan administration was more concentrated on terrorism than on the Middle East concerns that had dominated earlier US policy-makers' attention was a factor whose influence took some time to become salient: the profound change, lasting for all Reagan's time in office, in the supply and pricing of oil. For almost a decade after the 1973 Middle Eastern war, the group of oil-exporting states organized in OPEC and especially the Arab oil producers led by Saudi Arabia, had been principal movers and shakers of the world. Sheikh Yamani, as Saudi oil minister (until his sudden removal in 1986), was widely seen as bestriding the whole sphere of international politics. The decision-makers of greater powers tended to assume that their respective countries were helplessly 'over a barrel': a barrel of oil, whose inevitable price-range seemed for a time to be from $30 upwards, and which might be withheld, even at those prices, if political offence were given. The 'oil shocks' of 1973 and 1979 had been reinforced by the political shock of seeing a regime as strong as the Shah's appeared to be in early 1978 crumple within a year to revolutionary forces led by ayatollahs and mullahs. If dangers so exotic could turn what the US had earlier defined as an indispensable regional ally into an unpredictable adversary, might they not (it was widely argued) do as much damage, with equal speed, in Saudi Arabia and the smaller Gulf states, and would not that bring the Western industrialized world down to darkness and ruin? At the beginning of President Reagan's time in office that had looked not only like the most plausible danger facing the West but almost the only one, outside the European and North Asian theatres, serious enough to warrant actual combat intervention by Western forces. The transformation of the Rapid Deployment Force into the Central Command, fleshed out by various assigned divisions and so on, was (at least in terms of declaratory signals) a strong response to that sort of alarm.

Yet events up to the final Reagan exit went in directions that seemed destined to allow those decisions to remain, fortunately, in the realm of declaratory policy for relatively improbable future contingencies. The decline in world demand for oil (because of energy conservation and recession, plus the rise of the non-OPEC oil producers like Britain) produced by the early 1980s a world awash in a glut of oil. That had its own considerable problems, but they were quite different from those envisaged in the late 1970s. The decline in demand began to show up in the statistics by 1979, and the real price per barrel declined from 1981, well before the dramatic price collapse of early 1986, which for a time brought the cost in constant 1973 dollars down close to its level before the great initial price-hike, though it rose temporarily towards $21 a barrel in 1989. Moreover, the glut of the 1980s persisted despite the Iran–Iraq war, which had somewhat crippled the exporting capacities of both those major oil producers.

So from early in President Reagan's second term it was apparent that the diplomatic leverage of OPEC was not again, for the immediate future, likely to be what it had once been, and that the organization might indeed have trouble in maintaining enough cohesion to secure a reasonable share of the world market. A hypothesis even seemed possible that the world could get by, at least for a short time, without Persian Gulf oil if it had to. (In the late 1980s, OPEC's share of the world market was temporarily down to about 30 per cent, and that of the Persian Gulf members of OPEC down to about 22 per cent. If that quota were lost for a period, other producers seemed likely to be able to expand for a short time enough to make good the gap, especially given the quite large reserves held in some countries.) Thus the probability of the area engendering a catastrophic crisis in relations between the superpowers became inherently more remote, unless the outcome of the Iran–Iraq war had been to change the local balance in the Gulf. Not many people would have dared to predict, when the war began in September 1980, that it could be waged (for the most part at the technological level of the First World War, but with some sophisticated weaponry) for most of the decade without any notable increase in superpower tension and without any reduction in the world glut of oil. Through the same period, Soviet capacity to finance external adventures and clients was also directly reduced, since as much as 60 per cent of Soviet hard-currency earnings came from the sale of oil. Some estimates held that each dollar drop in price per barrel represented a loss of $500 million a year in the foreign exchange earnings at the disposal of policy-makers in Moscow.

Thus, though the temporary transformation in the world oil scene created major problems for some American friends (like Mexico and Venezuela) as well as in the 'oil patch' at home, it reduced the salience of possibilities and apprehensions that had dominated strategic and diplomatic speculation in the late 1970s and early 1980s, and which had seemed to some of Reagan's allies and critics to hint at the danger of rash American enterprises. For instance, the President had said in October 1981 at a press conference that the US 'would not permit Saudi Arabia to be another Iran'.[25] Since the forces of change in Iran had indubitably been domestic discontents, manipulated less successfully by the left than by Islamic fundamentalists, that seemed, if taken seriously, to mean that the US might intervene to repress forces of domestic revolutionary change directed against the Saudi regime. The implication was not gratefully received by the Saudi governing élite who pointed out, with some justification, that their situation was distinctly different from what the Shah's had been. It also caused much alarm and irritation elsewhere.

Even without taking such remarks seriously, the Reagan policies during this initial phase had to be seen as fashioned to convey a strong conscious signal of a turn away from the Carter preoccupation with Israeli–Arab relations towards re-emphasised preoccupation with the Soviet Union, depicted as presenting the most urgent danger to the region. The 'strategic consensus' to which Haig originally hoped to persuade the Arab Gulf states and others was to be a consensus on that analysis or viewpoint. But of course, the states which had to be persuaded remained preoccupied with the Iran–Iraq war, and with Israel, and with the defection of Egypt from the Arab cause as most of the other Arab states defined it. So the broad regional strategic consensus which was to have centred on Saudi Arabia came to little, except perhaps (unfortunately as it appeared during the Iran hearings) enhanced Israeli influence on American strategic assessments.

The Administration did have, however, a reasonable level of success in lining-up the sort of logistic facilities that would be helpful if push should ever come to shove in the Gulf area, and some more serious intervention by US air and naval forces were put in train. That meant cultivating in particular Pakistan and the Arab state of Oman whose territory commanded the entrance to the Persian Gulf. (Since the Sultan of Oman had recently been threatened by a rebellion in Dofar backed by a Soviet ally, South Yemen, he was more unequivocally pro-Western than most Arab decision-makers. Also the area was an old British protectorate and British influence remained strong, especially in the Omani armed forces.) The British island of Diego Garcia, in the middle of the Indian Ocean, was transformed into a substantial staging base: arrangements with Australia were secured for routeing aircraft from Guam in the Pacific through Darwin in North Australia round to Diego Garcia and northward if necessary, perhaps to Masirah Island off Oman: naval arrangements were made with Kenya and Somalia for facilities in case US ships had to be sent up the coast of East Africa towards the Gulf. Most of the facilities secured were rather remote from the Gulf itself, except those in Oman, yet these well-publicized arrangements were in themselves loud declaratory signals, and not necessarily ineffective. The same might be said of the explicit cultivation of relations with Pakistan, and the quite overt pipeline of US supplies (including by 1986 Stinger ground-to-air missiles) through Pakistan to Afghanistan. The often-debated notion that Soviet strategic planners might have had in mind a long-term project of carving out and sponsoring an independent state of Baluchistan, which would allow Soviet forces to move from Afghanistan down to a port on the Arabian Sea (near the mouth of the Persian Gulf), possibly never had much substance to it. But if it did, one could say that the prospect of strong American resistance was assiduously signalled from the earliest days of the Reagan Administration, as it had been in the final Carter year.

An equally notable element in American Middle Eastern policy in the Reagan years was a tendency for US–Israeli relations to develop a heavy load of ambiguities and to move up and down like a roller-coaster. A down-phase began early, with Israeli intransigence in 1981 over Washington's efforts (particularly those of Weinberger) to cultivate ties with Saudi Arabia. If the Israelis had some reason for suspicion of Washington, the policy-makers there could claim cause for alarm at some of the policies of their Israeli ally, whose chief decision-maker at this period, Menachem Begin, had already demonstrated a truly formidable capacity for recalcitrance during his negotiations with Carter and Sadat at Camp David. The difference in priorities between the new policy-makers in Washington and those in Israel dominated the arguments over getting an AWACS deal with Saudi Arabia through Congress. That issue was a matter of political importance for the President as a symbol of his general capacity to control US policy, and it rapidly proved one in which Mr Begin was determined to be no help at all. At the period when the President was trying to convince the Senate that the Saudi élite were moderates and an influence for peace in the Middle East, Mr Begin was vigorously denouncing them to American-Jewish organizations as mediaeval, despotic, corrupt and supporters of terrorism. There was also his assiduous pressing forward of Israeli settlements on the West Bank, with the obvious implication of potential annexation. Moreover, the Israeli air-strike in June 1981 at the nuclear reactor in Iraq, though rationalized as a measure of self-defence in Israeli arguments, was regarded as an unnecessary piece of strong-arm tactics by most expert opinion in the US, which held at the time that the Iraqis were ten years from a practicable bomb. There were Israeli air-strikes also at the Palestine Liberation Organization in Lebanon and Tunisia, one of which was reported to have killed over 300 civilians. Moreover, Mr Begin rushed through the Knesset a measure which amounted to *de facto* annexation of the Golan Heights, without prior information to Washington.

Much worse was the situation through most of 1982, with the Israeli invasion of Lebanon. It was widely believed in the Arab world that Washington had accepted the Israeli decision with a shrug or had even encouraged it. The account given in Haig's memoirs does not support this, but there does seem to have been undue optimism in Washington as well as Israel that the episode could be quickly and cleanly over, a view which proved to be an illusion. The war did not for long achieve even its primary objectives, the expulsion of the PLO from Lebanon and its destruction as a military force. Less than four years later, by early 1986, the PLO (though still divided) were again encamped in Southern Lebanon in some strength, in the Arkoub Valley and near Sidon and Tyre. Yasser Arafat was again more or less in charge, with financial support still from Saudi Arabia. The Israeli occupation area in Lebanon and even the villages in Galilee were again under attack. The Islamic fundamentalists of Hezbollah, who look for inspiration to the Ayatollah Khomeini, were gaining influence among the Shiah population of South Lebanon, and seemed likely to prove more dangerous and determined in suicide attacks than the PLO. Still more damaging, the longer-term changes produced in Lebanon by the Israeli invasion were of a sort unlikely to prove helpful either to Israel or to the US. The chances of a strong central government based on the Christian factions, and able to assert their independence of Syria, had been reduced to vanishing point. The future of Lebanon looked to be that of a Syrian sphere of influence, in a state of endemic internal war between armed militias addicted to hostage-taking, with local politics dominated by the Muslim majority, especially the Shiah, and the Christian factions restricted to 'mini-states' in a system of *de facto* 'cantonization'.

Moreover, even the most confirmed of Israel's friends in the West had blanched at the reports of the massacres (which seemed to have been permitted by Israeli military authorities) in the Sabra and Chatila camps in Beirut. No doubt they were the result of the vengeful hatreds of Lebanese factional politics, but a government which has sent its army to occupy a neighbouring country cannot escape blame for what happens under the aegis of those occupying forces. Television pictures of the chaos and destruction in Lebanon dominated the evening news in the US for many months. Casualties to Israeli's armed forces were heavy by Israeli standards (about 650 dead), and the sense of being sent to fight an unpopular or unjustifiable war was psychologically damaging to young Israeli soldiers, as it had been to their American equivalents in Vietnam. So altogether, at some years' retrospect, the invasion of Lebanon had to be seen as the least successful of Israel's wars, damaging not only to Lebanon and to Israel itself, but in the longer run to the American capacity, at least for the Reagan term, to advance the peace process in the area. It did, however, provide a reminder of the instability of the Middle East and the dangers of inaction, and thus forced some shift in Washington's preoccupations from the Persian Gulf and Libyan ends of the Middle Eastern imbroglio back to the Arab–Israeli confrontation that remained at its heart.

In a sense, the delay of the Administration in taking up that particular burden was not surprising in terms of party-political feeling. Camp David had been the one acclaimed foreign-policy achievement of the Carter Administration, building on the earlier Kissinger success in the step-by-step disengagement process over the Sinai. Those were not names pronounced with any notable enthusiasm in the early months of the Reagan first term. Besides, even if the Democratic administration had been returned to power, it was not clear that there would have been many prospects, for the time being, of advancing the peace process. Israeli opinion (and American–Jewish opinion) were already profoundly ambivalent or divided about the actual consequences for Israel's security of any further moves in the general technique of trading occupied territory for diplomatic agreements. Furthermore, the assassination of President Sadat of Egypt in 1981 not only removed the most important of America's remaining friends in the Arab world, it indicated the dangers with which any Arab statesman was confronted who chose to put his life on the line in pursuit of objectives opposed by Moslem militants. President Mubarak as Sadat's successor had a pressing political need to orientate himself rather to rebuilding the Egyptian role in the Middle East and Africa. The stationing of the Marines in Beirut in the aftermath of the Israeli military action produced the most costly American casualty list of any US military operation in the Reagan years: 241 dead in the car-bomb explosion of 1983, along with others killed in smaller incidents or held as hostages, some of the latter remaining in captivity for years and eventually inspiring the intended deals with Iran which ultimately proved, for a time, almost as damaging to the prestige and morale of the Administration as the earlier Iran hostage crisis had been to Jimmy Carter's.

The 'Reagan Plan' for the Middle East, put forward in September 1982 in unpromising circumstances, amounted more or less to an elaboration of the 'Jordanian solution' which had been canvassed by assorted policy-makers and scholarly authorities at intervals for almost ten years. It called for a federated Jordan–Palestine state to incorporate the West Bank and Gaza Strip and co-exist with Israel. Shultz had replaced Haig as Secretary of State in the middle of the Lebanon crisis, and possibly that change promoted a larger role in policy-making for the Middle Eastern hands in the State Department, Shultz being much more a 'team player' than some of his predecessors, and more inclined to allow a strong role to the bureaucracy. Almost a year earlier, in October 1981, the Saudis had put forward the 'Fahd plan', which had called for a Palestinian state in the West Bank and Gaza, with East Jerusalem as its capital: Israeli withdrawal from all occupied territories, the right of Palestinians to repatriation, and a temporary UN trusteeship for the transition period. None of that was acceptable to Israel, and therefore US endorsement was never possible, but its brushing aside by the Reagan proposals was not calculated to sweeten relations with the Arabs. When George Bush visited Saudi Arabia several years later, in April 1986, he got a distinct 'cold shoulder' from the Saudi decision-makers, partly for some tactlessly expressed views on the fall in oil prices, but also because of this earlier US snub, plus the agonizing slowness and only partial success of the Administration in getting the approval of Congress for proposed arms deals for Saudi Arabia and Jordan. (Israeli lobbying against them had been substantially successful.) Instead of a fly-past of American F–5s and F–15s, the Saudis (as a heavy hint to their US guest) arranged a fly-past of their new Tornadoes, part of a $4–6 billion arms deal with Britain. A still larger arms deal was concluded by the Saudis with Britain in 1988, and many other Arab arms-buyers also sought alternative suppliers, thus, in the upshot, considerably reducing American leverage in any future crisis.

All the Arab oil-producers, including the Saudis, were by the mid-1980s conscious that their own diplomatic leverage, at least for the rest of the Reagan period, had also been much reduced by the oil glut. Furthermore, governmental incomes in the area had fallen with devastating speed, while the ambitious welfare systems those governments had set up at the peak of national affluence were still as expensive as ever. OPEC was for a time barely able to hold together enough to attempt some control over ceilings for oil production. Iraq had needed to be sustained for most of the period, lest the Ayatollah should achieve a victory which would encourage Shiah assertiveness in the Gulf states. All the Arabs had been tarred with the terrorist brush in the eyes of American public opinion, and that meant that further US arms sales had great difficulty making their way through Congress, despite such efforts as the Administration persisted in making.

Since Arab diplomatic leverage in Washington was by 1985 conspicuously down, Israeli morale and influence were for a time erratically but very conspicuously up. In 1982 so well-informed an 'insider' as Joseph Sisco could write that US–Israeli relations were 'more difficult than at any time since 1956' (when Eisenhower and Dulles had forced the Israelis out of Sinai and the Gaza Strip). In 1986, by contrast, another very well informed 'insider', Richard B. Strauss, could write that opinion in the Administration and on Capitol Hill had shifted so radically in favour of Israel that the skilled Israeli lobby AIPAC (America–Israel Public Affairs Committee) no longer had to exert itself. Previously its job had been 'to lobby the Congress to tell the President to overrule the State Department'. But neither Congress nor the Secretary of State any longer needed much persuasion.[26] The experiences of Mr Shultz in the Middle Eastern capitals were reportedly crucial in this shift. At the time when he replaced Haig in 1982 and assumed responsibility for the initiative which turned into the Reagan peace plan of September, the assumption had been, from his past affiliation with Bechtel, that he might be rather more sympathetic to the Arab cause than the Israelis would like. But by early 1984, reportedly, when he had emerged from the Lebanon débâcle he felt 'betrayed by the moderate Arabs, notably the Saudis, and humiliated by the radicals, namely Syria'.[27]

That was the background against which the Israeli involvement, along with the US, in the Iran-Nicaragua arms imbroglio has to be seen. There did not seem any doubt (especially after the Tower Commission report) that Colonel North and Admiral Poindexter were influenced by Israeli policy-makers and intelligence analysts in the whole development of the project from its earliest days, and consciousness of this fact cast a somewhat dubious light on the estimates of the Iranian political situation by which Robert McFarlane and others were guided (or misguided) in their original approach to Teheran. There is, and has long been, a clear difference of strategic interests between the US and Israel as regards Iran. Because of the bitterness and prospectively long-enduring nature of Israel's quarrel with the Arab states, Israeli governments up till the fall of the Shah in 1979 had been accustomed to see Iran, which also had tensions with its Arab neighbours, especially Iraq, as at least an occasional co-belligerent against the Arab enemy. Even the rise of the Ayatollah and Islamic fundamentalism did not altogether undermine that viewpoint: there was always the hope that the fundamentalist élan would dissipate itself with the Ayatollah's death and Iran would return to some approximation of its earlier attitudes before his rise. Israel did not have interests and quasi-allies to protect in the Gulf as the US did in Saudi Arabia and the small Arab oil-producing states. So it was possible to see the Iran imbroglio as the outcome of National Security Council officials unwarily accepting the guidance of sharper-witted and better-informed agents of Mossad, the Israeli intelligence service, in an area in which US interests diverged visibly from those of Israel.

By a painful coincidence, the US had at the same time another reason for resentment at the operations of the Israeli intelligence services: the case of Jonathan Jay Pollard, who was sentenced to life imprisonment (and his wife to five years in gaol) for passing to Israel copies of secret documents that came his way during his work in naval intelligence. The Israeli Foreign Minister, Shimon Peres, apologized and said it would not happen again. But the Israeli secret agents who had recruited Pollard and handled his material were promoted. And in another case which offended American moral feeling, the beating to death of two Arab prisoners who had been in the hands of the Israeli security service, Shin Beth, those responsible were again protected.

Well before some of these events, the elements which made up the Iran–Contra arms imbroglio were beginning to come together in Washington and Jerusalem and other locales. If there is a single clue to the unfolding of so apparently unlikely a series of events, it may be found in one of the Middle Eastern hostages, who had an overwhelming claim on the best efforts of the CIA to retrieve him. That was William Buckley, who had been kidnapped in March 1984 by Islamic Jihad and who had been the CIA station chief in Beirut. His colleagues in Washington had to assume that he was under torture to force him to disclose the names of other American agents in the area. Since he died in the hands of his captors that bleak assumption was probably the correct one. But as long as he was believed alive, William Casey as head of the CIA and an old 'field operative' of the Office of Strategic Studies (OSS) was under the heaviest moral pressure to do all that could be done towards his rescue including, if necessary, breaking quite a few legal rules. Perhaps Casey felt in addition the special freedom from constraints that came from knowing he was himself stricken with cancer and might not have long to go (he actually died of a brain tumour during the early months of the investigation, in May 1987). Also he was no doubt considerably irked by the Congressional restraints that had been placed on CIA operations and conscious that these constraints did not apply to the NSC, since that had never been classed as an intelligence agency. So in the Iran arms imbroglio its ex-chief, Robert McFarlane, and some of its current officials, including Colonel North, were recruited to a covert intelligence operation. The CIA's most hopeful channel into Iran, in early 1985, was through the help of an Israeli, Yaacov Nimrodi, who had been the chief agent of Mossad, the Israeli intelligence service, in Teheran for fourteen years, mostly in the Shah's time, and still had his contacts there. The Iranian who was found to make an approach to the government in Iran was an arms-dealer, Manuchar Ghorbanifar. The signal that came back from Teheran (not from 'moderates' but from the Prime Minister) was of the pressing need for TOW anti-tank missiles to use in the war against Iraq. Six hundred were delivered in August and September and perhaps helped determine one battle, though obviously not the war. William Buckley, of course, was not retrieved. But Oliver North convinced himself and some of his superiors that it would be 'a neat idea' to fund arms for the Contras from the profits of the sales to the Ayatollah.

So much has been already written about what followed that it seems unnecessary to add much more here. The episode will perhaps not retain as dominant a place in final assessments of the balance sheet of President Reagan's foreign policy as once seemed likely. Its basic elements were, however, entirely characteristic of the Administration's overall style, like a caricature that catches a personality by exaggerating its traits. Most notably, of course, the gap between declaratory and operational policy, into which Presidential credibility fell. The President's own administrative stance was so laid-back by that phase of his Administration as to allow even a 'by-the-book, chain-of-command' personality like Admiral Poindexter to assume, after only two months in office, that he should keep from his Commander-in-Chief so important a detail as the diversion of the Ayatollah's funds to the Contras. (The influence of the intelligence concept of 'plausible deniability' was obviously strong there.) So 'one confused lieutenant-colonel', as Oliver North apologetically described himself, ended up running an important segment of US foreign policy. Two of the President's own embargoes (or at any rate declaratory policies) were broken: those enjoining no US arms for the Iran–Iraq war and no dealings with terrorists. And all to very little effect: the hostages were not retrieved, or those that were let out were replaced by others; the Contras did not get much in the way of funds. No channels were opened up to the assumed 'moderates': in fact, it seems possible that the Ayatollah himself authorized creation of an impression that such a group was sending signals from Teheran in order to acquire the missiles. American embarrassment at the failure of the rescue efforts, and a wish to retrieve credit with the Arabs, helped to induce Washington to lurch into the 'reflagging' operation for tankers, which for a time entailed a considerably raised level of costs and risks in the Gulf.

During the final Reagan year, these naval operations in the Gulf were watched with considerable apprehension by Washington's European allies and by the Arab world. Among their costs, in human terms, was the tragic death-toll in the accidental destruction of an Iranian airliner in July 1988 by a US warship. Nevertheless, the final reluctant acceptance of a cease-fire by Iran probably owed something to Teheran's reading of the signals from Washington as implying a ruthless American determination that it would not be allowed to win, so possibly it was in the upshot warranted.

In the conflict between Israel and its Arab neighbours, the final few Reagan weeks saw the pressures for change developing a 'critical mass' that could produce another explosion. Alternatively, if adroitly managed by the Bush policy-makers in this area, it might help move the peace process along a hard-fought notch or two, despite Israeli mistrust. A new fluidity marked the stances of several of the key players in the Middle Eastern drama. The decision of the outgoing Reagan policymakers, in their last month or so, to open talks with the PLO undoubtedly helped free the hands of their Washington successors. It also brought US–Israeli relations to a lower point than any of the other episodes mentioned in this chapter. Memories of an earlier crisis-point, 1956–7, and the tough-mindedness with which another newly-elected Republican, Eisenhower, jockeyed Israeli occupying forces out of Gaza and the Sinai are bound to hang over the impending discussions of the future of Gaza and the West Bank. The sight of Israeli troops, on the nightly TV news, 'dealing with' the intifada, as embodied in stone-throwing children, sharply reduced the normal level of warm approval felt for Israel as an American ally. The apparent intransigence of the Prime Minister and Foreign Minister (Yitzak Shamir and Moshe Arens) did nothing to retrieve the damage. The successful travels of the Soviet Foreign Minister in the Middle East in February and March, along with the strong signals from the Europeans (especially Britain) increased the necessity for a new American initiative. The direction of pressure could hardly be other than towards Israeli concessions that would permit the creation of a truncated Palestine from the West Bank and the Gaza Strip. Thus from the earliest Bush months the prospect of a new (and to the Israelis probably rather agonizing) spasm of the Middle Eastern drama was clear.

6. Third World: The 'Reagan Doctrine' and a Confounding of Assumptions

The image of Reagan administration policies in the Third World, other than the Middle East, was inevitably dominated by the operations in Nicaragua (especially after the publicizing of the illegal diversion of funds to the Contras from the Iran arms sales) and by some unduly optimistic and ambitious accounts of the alleged successes and potentialities of the 'Reagan Doctrine'. But what seems to emerge on examination of actual developments in this enormous and disparate field of US policy-making is how little the final outcomes matched the initial assumptions. That applies to the initial assumptions of the liberal critics of the Reagan policies (who originally wrote as if they expected the Reagan years to confirm in power every right-wing authoritarian US client government) as well as to neo-conservative enthusiasts for the Reagan aspirations (who at one stage, late in 1985, seemed to believe they had found a magic technique in 'the Reagan Doctrine' for disposing of every left-wing totalitarian Soviet-oriented government in the Third World.) Those hopes were exaggerated, despite Afghanistan and Angola, but so equally, or even more completely, were the pessimists' assumptions that every illiberal regime would be confirmed in power. In fact, the casualty rate among such regimes, right or left, from various causes during the Reagan years was remarkably high. Even the long-established tough-minded autocracies of Paraguay and Chile were shaken. The Philippines, South Korea, Taiwan, Haiti, Argentina, Grenada, Brazil, Honduras, Bolivia, Guatemala, Uruguay and Panama all had by 1988 seen a discrediting of 'strong man' governments, and some Washington influences (though not necessarily the President's) had helped amplify the 'winds of change' involved. Washington's South African policy had also moved in directions that seemed as surprising to some supporters of the Administration as they were disconcerting to the South African regime.

Understanding what happened turns again on the distinction between declaratory and operational policy. In this particular field, the initial declaratory policy appeared to imply solid, set-in-concrete attitudes of benign tolerance for authoritarian allies in the Third World. Professor Jeane Kirkpatrick, writing in 1979 as an academic in an article in *Commentary* during the Reagan battle for nomination,[28] had proposed a distinction that Mr Reagan as a presidential candidate found useful for his potential Third World policies: a distinction between 'authoritarian' and 'totalitarian' regimes. Making a plausible argument on this question was much more important for right-wing than for left-liberal doctrine. The liberal candidate may be able to proclaim bold sweeping condemnations (at least before he encounters the compromises of office) of both those varieties of non-democratic regimes, on the reasonable ground that they deny or frustrate the will of the people, which can only be discerned and checked by free, fair and regular elections and by conceding the legitimacy of opposition. That position was more difficult to maintain, even in theory, for those close enough to office to be conscious that the US had quite a few strategically useful allies and client states in the Third World whose governments were insecure military autocracies (as in much of Latin America at the time) or personal autocracies (as in the Philippines or Haiti at the time and as had been the case earlier in Iran with the Shah). Totalitarian governments, in the most useful usage of the term, are those which seek to monopolize control over the *totality* of life in the society they have seized, including economic, religious and cultural matters. Authoritarian governments merely seek to monopolize *authority*, or political power, leaving the existing economy, social structure and cultural or religious patterns largely to tradition or market forces. By the Reagan period, totalitarian regimes were more or less coterminous with communist regimes, though one might make a case that Islamic fundamentalist regimes (as in Iran) are also in the literal sense totalitarian, as, of course, had been the Nazi and Fascist regimes of the 1930s. Jimmy Carter's human rights campaign had, on the evidence, proved damaging (though not necessarily by intent) to two personal autocracies – that of the Shah and that of Somoza (who were both overthrown in 1979) – but totally ineffective against the dogmatic party-based totalitarian systems of the communist world. And, of course, the falls both of the Shah and of Somoza had created conditions for the emergence of new regimes (in Iran, the Ayatollah's Islamic fundamentalism, and in Nicaragua, the Sandinista's Cuba-modelled communism) which had not only become dangerous enemies of the United States, but appeared ambitious to export their doctrines throughout their respective neighbourhoods: the Persian Gulf in the Iranian Case, and the Caribbean and Central America in the Nicaraguan case. Moreover, one could define the change as being from authoritarian to totalitarian in both cases, and thus, at least in neo-conservative doctrine, see it as reducing the chances of future evolution towards a true pluralist democracy in either case.

Jeane Kirkpatrick's area of academic interest had been Latin America, so with her appointment to the UN Ambassadorship, and the publication of a further *Commentary* article indicating a policy for that region,[29] it was widely assumed that her theory would provide the broad intellectual guideline for Reagan policies for the Third World, especially areas of traditional interest to the United States like Latin America and the Philippines, and that such policies would include considerable sympathy and propping-up for any endangered authoritarian friends, as well as more serious efforts at 'rollback' of communist gains in areas of American interest.

Grenada certainly, and more broadly the Caribbean and Central America as a whole, must be construed as having seen efforts at 'rollbacks' of earlier communist gains. Support for the Contras in Nicaragua and for the guerrilla insurgencies in Angola, Kampuchea and Afghanistan (all overtly or covertly supplied by the US) might plausibly be classed as strong signals of the Administration's resolve not to permit a consolidation of communist power in still-contested areas.

The rationale for changes in US attitudes on Third World questions was in some quasi-official or journalistic quarters presented as 'the Reagan Doctrine', either for purposes of praise or blame.[30] In actuality, that name seemed somewhat of a misnomer, flatteringly intended. Policy change derived less from the President himself than from a perception, apparently by middle-level policy-makers, that what had been sauce for the right-wing goose might be made to cook the left-wing gander, at least in the Third World. That is, that US policy, instead of wasting resources on efforts at repressing dissent against shaky right-wing autocracies (a cause which had so often proved expensive, unpopular and finally lost), should instead devote resources to backing or accommodating to dissent and insurgencies directed against both varieties of non-democratic regimes, though, of course, especially those directed against shaky left-wing regimes allied to the Soviet Union. Strategic considerations alone would not necessarily have required acquiescing in, still less helping along, popular movements against right-wing regimes which (though discreditable by democratic standards) had earlier been classed as useful or essential allies. Nevertheless, by 1987 for those who had observed the changing signals on Haiti, the Philippines and South Africa, it seemed reasonable to surmise that, accidentally or otherwise, the Administration had come round to policies whose impact on allies as important as Taiwan or South Korea might be quite far-reaching, as proved indeed the case. For when you are proclaiming, as Mr Shultz did, that 'the yearning for freedom is the most powerful political force all across the planet' there is no way to ensure that the message reaches only countries where the repressive regime in power is rationalized by left-wing doctrines rather than right-wing ones.

One of the factors behind the change was the bureaucratic recognition in Washington that whereas even a decade earlier most of the insurgencies round the world were left-wing movements operating against right-wing governments, by the mid-1980s that was no longer true. Marxist regimes (and other varieties of socialism, as in Burma) had proven just as capable as capitalist ones of making themselves unpopular, especially with their peasantries; and given the necessary kind of geographical assets (mountains, jungles, dense bush) insurgencies had proved just as able to base themselves on Muslim doctrines or right-wing nationalisms or economic discontent as on left-wing ideologies. In fact, by 1985 many of the larger insurgencies round the globe were directed against Marxist or quasi-Marxist governments: the Mujahaddin in Afghanistan, Savimbi's forces in Angola, the Contras in Nicaragua, the mixed bag of anti-Vietnamese forces in Kampuchea, and the Eritreans in Ethiopia. (The Renamo dissidents in Mozambique, though also operating against a feebly Marxist regime, seem to have been regarded less favourably in

Washington, for reasons to do with their South African connections and with atrocities on their part.) Policy-makers in Washington could hopefully regard the new US stance as prospectively more 'cost-effective' than the old, since it is considerably less expensive to subsidize guerrillas than to support besieged governments. It appeared not without logic as a stratagem in the general conflict with the Soviet Union. Moreover, some weapons developments, especially the Stinger surface-to-air missile, had shown promise of altering the military balance in favour of the guerrillas, by wiping out the advantages of air-cover and helicopter gun-ships, as in Afghanistan.

The Clark Amendment, which in 1975 had prohibited the expenditure of funds to assist the anti-communist factions in Angola (and which had at the time expressed the overwhelming fear in Congress of 'another Vietnam'), was repealed in mid-1985 without any real difficulty and with some Democratic support in Congress: a striking signal of the change in US national mood. The President himself seemed rather slow to appreciate the two-edged potential of the doctrine marketed under his name, remarking in May 1983 that the treatment of guerrillas 'should be based on what kind of government they are opposing', meaning, presumably, that they should only be supported if they were fighting America's enemies. But by 1988 one could certainly say that as many right-wing as left-wing regimes had proved vulnerable to their oppositions, though not necessarily always with as much administration enthusiasm from Washington.

The departure of President Marcos from the Philippines in early 1986 offered a clear case study. If one puts the question, Did he fall or was he pushed? the answer given by Ferdinand Marcos himself was a vehement insistence that he was indeed pushed, by assorted Washington hands. In an interview in his Hawaiian exile he maintained that there had been a direct American role in a conspiracy for a *coup d'état*, and even that the conspiracy had included plans to assassinate both himself and Imelda. He also insisted that the Americans had deceived him about his destination when he was persuaded to leave the Malacanang Palace: intending to go to his home province of Ilocos Norte he found himself taken instead to Guam and on to Hawaii. President Reagan, he implied, had been misled by a faction in the US bureaucracy and factions in the US media. 'The US has become a country of trial by publicity.[31] (In 1987 his apparent plot to return was also foiled by US agents and by 1988 he and his wife were on trial in the US.)

The Marcos analysis, of course, was obviously self-serving and calculated to minimize the true role of Filipino opinion. His twenty-year regime took the final down-turn to its ultimate ruin more than two years before the end, with the assassination of Benigno Aquino and the emergence in due course of his widow, Corazon Aquino, as a focus of all the dissent and resentments of those Filipinos who could neither adhere to the Communists nor continue to acquiesce in the rule of the President and his cronies. In particular, the murder alienated two powerful forces which were to prove decisive in the final showdown: the Church and a section of the armed forces. The Church could not tolerate so blatant a resort to official killing for political purposes. Some of the Army generals, those who were not adherents of the men immediately round the President, could not blind themselves to the certainty of connivance at the murder among some of their senior colleagues and were angered at the damage to the reputation of their profession.

So the prime moving forces of the revolt against Marcos were undoubtedly generated in the Philippines, especially among the middle classes and a section of the political élite in Manila. But as to the signals which, in effect, brought down the avalanche and to some extent guided its direction, evidence independent of ex-President Marcos shows a considerable input not from President Reagan himself but from the Washington establishment. In particular, it was from an assumed necessity to convince Washington that he still had the mandate of the people that President Marcos decided to hold the snap election which proved the occasion of his undoing. The decision was even announced in Washington, during a Marcos press conference on television. There had earlier, in October, been a visit to Manila by Senator Paul Laxalt (who was not only a powerful figure on Capitol Hill but a close friend of President Reagan), during which Marcos was reportedly told, in effect, that it might be time for him to go or at least that reforms must be made if his regime was to remain effective, particularly in view of the growing strength of the Communist insurgency. Its military wing, the New People's Army (NPA), was at that time estimated to number between 16 000 and 20 000 men under arms, and to have been causing about 1500 deaths a year by its operations during the period immediately before Marcos's downfall. Its mass base was among the bitterly poor peasantry, especially in agriculturally distressed regions. Whether (and how fast) any government in Manila could institute the sort of sweeping reforms in land tenure and rural social structure necessary to undermine the NPA's power of recruitment and operations was judged by Washington experts in Philippines questions to be a matter of great uncertainty, but the prospects without such change had by late 1985 come to appear clearly disastrous to many policy-makers in Washington.

The necessity of securing reform in the armed forces as well as the political and economic systems was also held to warrant radical measures, such as were in due course taken. Some elements in the Filipino army had from 1977 been growing discontented with General Ver and the elderly cohort of officers who were being allowed to run the armed forces. By the time of the crisis, this rebellious-minded faction was expecting a crackdown from Marcos and Ver, which might have put many of its members in gaol or underground. The decision to throw their support behind Cory Aquino was therefore not surprising, even for those whose earlier records did not exactly qualify them as ardent democrats. General Ver received a sharp signal from the National Security Council in Washington that it would 'not be to his interest' to attempt to order his troops to fire on the crowds, as he seemed to be deliberately threatening to do during the last Marcos TV conference (that is, he was given to understand that such an action would prejudice his hopes of sanctuary in the US). Similar messages seem to have gone from US sources to other Marcos adherents still in command of troops in the final week of the crisis. So one can say that Washington's vigorous crisis-management seems to have played a decisive role in the process of persuasion or coercion which prevented a bloodbath, though feelings among the troops themselves, and on Marcos's own part, were also inhibiting factors on any attempt at the military repression of 'people power'.

Possibly Moscow accidentally strengthened Washington's hand in that bit of arm-twisting. It not only congratulated Marcos on 'winning' the election, it had *Pravda* put out a story, just before the crisis-resolution, that a coup was planned against Marcos, probably with CIA participation. So Moscow's signals conceivably operated to reinforce Washington's indications that it was time for him to make an exit, with the implication that if it was not by means of a helicopter to Clark Field it might be by means of a bullet. Nevertheless, a couple of final Washington signals were required to convince Marcos or his wife: the telephone conversation with Senator Laxalt just a few hours before he opted for the helicopter to Clark Field, and the very strong signal conveyed by an intimation that President Reagan would not receive Marcos's own telephone call.

It was very much a 'revolution of the centre', not of the left. Not only the communists but other left-leaning groups had advised Filipino voters to boycott the elections. Thus, one initial political effect of the unexpected success of Cory Aquino appeared to be to reduce the prestige and attraction of left-wing doctrines or parties, at least among middle-class groups like students and perhaps among the urban poor. However, it was impossible to say for how long this effective competition with the left's appeal would last, unless the new government were able to score more major successes than appeared at all likely.

The changes in American policy, on the evidence at present available, stemmed less from the President than what I have called the Washington establishment: high bureaucrats, powerful Congressmen and Senators, and influential media figures. Senators Laxalt, Solarz and Lugar and, in the bureaucracy, Paul Wolfowitz (at the time Assistant Secretary of State for Asia and the Far East), Michael Armacost (former Ambassador in Manila) and Richard Armitage (Deputy Secretary of Defense) played important roles, along with Philip Habib, who was the State Department's intermediary with both sides in Manila and who was reported to have told the Washington crisis-managers a couple of days before the end that 'the Marcos regime is over'. The television and newspaper editors who kept a relentless American spotlight on events in Manila throughout the election undoubtedly also played a vital role both in generating the crisis and in determining its outcome. The fact that the campaign and the election itself were not free and fair but, on the contrary, subject to quite ludicrously blatant 'rigging' could not be concealed or passed over because of the presence on the scene not only of the American media *en masse* but the official observers. President Reagan's personal signals, almost until the final days, did not seem to show any clear understanding on his part either of what was happening in the Philippines or even of what his own policy-makers were doing.

The change of government in the Philippines did not end the problems the area presented for Washington policy-makers. Hostilities with the communist insurgents resumed after an attempt at a truce, and the army remained so racked with dissidence that there were five coup attempts in the first eighteen months. Assorted question-marks remained over the future of Clark Field and Subic Bay after 1991.

The example of events in the Philippines had a clear impact on the regimes in power in South Korea and Taiwan and on their respective oppositions or dissentients, making those who wanted change more optimistic and activist and those who held power more conscious that the time to yield might be at hand. Both of those societies, unlike the Philippines, had enjoyed over the past few decades amazing rates of economic growth, among the highest in the world. In both cases that process had created a large, technically-sophisticated middle class, and a large student class (about 30 per cent of the relevant age-group in South Korea) who could readily act as the shock troops of democratic revolution. In fact, a few weeks of student rioting in South Korea combined with Washington signals of the need for change (which had been conveyed from behind the scenes from at least 1986 and more strongly and publicly from early 1987 in, for instance, the speeches of the Assistant Secretary of State for East Asian and Pacific Affairs, Gaston Sigur) undoubtedly had some effect. They were no doubt reinforced by the more open pressures of Senator Edward Kennedy, among others, and by the extra media attention generated by the impending Olympic Games.

The changes in Taiwan were more elementary and attracted much less world attention, but the suspension of martial law for the first time in 37 years and the legitimation (within strict limits) of opposition did seem to indicate the beginnings of a political movement in the direction of liberalization, if not actual democracy. There was also a marked loosening of the restrictions on dealings with Communist China, and Chiang Ching-Kuo's successor as President was the Taiwan-born Lee Teng-hui, an omen of the inevitable phasing-out with age of the 'mainlander' élite.

Whereas the President's personal input into the turn of events in the Philippines and East Asia had seemed minimal, on Nicaragua it appeared tremendous. Preoccupation with the small states of Central America and the even smaller ones of the Caribbean tended to be regarded by many of America's allies as a sort of irrational personal Reagan neurosis. That was a somewhat mistaken view, since plenty of Presidential precedents existed for such attitudes. President Johnson in 1965, during the crisis over the Dominican Republic, for instance, was equally vehement over a similar issue, saying that the US could not, must not and would not allow another communist government to come to power in the Western hemisphere. And he used direct military force (about 25 000 troops) to overthrow the regime concerned. By comparison with that episode, or with the 1954 invasion of Guatemala in Eisenhower's time or the 1961 Bay of Pigs fiasco in Kennedy's time, the Reagan policies in Nicaragua predominantly relied on heavy signalling and the sustenance of local insurgents, not on actual combat operations involving US forces. The tradition of endemic Presidential heavy-handedness in that part of the world must be traced at least back to the Teddy Roosevelt corollary of the Monroe Doctrine. In that President's time, assertive policies in the Caribbean and Central America had the strategic rationale of an assumed need to get the US fleet from the Atlantic to the Pacific in secure conditions at times of crisis. In the nuclear age, that previously-assumed vital interest had ceased to be of much importance, but the route through Panama did remain vital in a logistic sense for the transport, for instance, of oil from Alaska across to the east coast ports, and the sort of military goods from the West Coast that would be going to Europe in time of crisis.

The initial declaratory signals from the Reagan policy-makers on Central American issues were particularly fierce, especially in defining Havana as the primary source of trouble, but even in the earliest days the operational signals did not quite match them. Ronald Reagan as candidate had, for instance, opposed the Panama Canal treaties, yet they were allowed to stay in force, a first indication of the gap between rhetoric and policy. But as a countervailing signal there was the apparent influence of the 'Committee of Santa Fé, whose report published in 1980[32] had propounded the view that a Third World War was already under way, with Latin America (and more especially Central America) viewed as the 'soft underbelly' of the United States, and thus the target at which the initial attack was being directed. Several of the report's originators (General Gordon Sumner, Roger Fontaine, Lewis Tombs) were recruited to the new Administration, another apparent indication of a tougher stance. Complementarily, quite a few of the State Department career people who had earlier specialized in Latin America found themselves deployed to other regions, and Thomas O. Enders, who had been a South-East Asian and NATO specialist, became the first of a succession of new bureaucratic policy-makers for the area. He was not a particularly ideological figure, but such appointments and removals seemed to reinforce the declaratory signals that neo-conservatives, or adherents of assorted other far-right ideologies, would be particularly in command on Latin America. As one official somewhat cynically put it:

> you've got to feed your right-wing somewhere. Maybe you'll just let them eat up Latin America. Its cheaper than some other places like the Middle East, the Soviet Union or China. . . . Just feed it to the lions.[33]

By early 1983 any initial expectations that the implied change of approach would produce rapid improvement in Central America had already come to seem doubtful in the eyes of some close Reagan aides such as Jeane Kirkpatrick and William Clark (then National Security Adviser). There ensued further personnel changes, so that by the time the Iran–Contra events were underway, the Assistant Secretary of State for Inter-American Affairs was Eliott Abrams, who was more closely identified with neo-conservative opinion than most of the Department of State specialists. Their position had tended to be that though the then-existing insurgencies in El Salvador and Guatemala could be defeated, the Marxist regime in Nicaragua should merely be 'contained', since defeating it would absorb too many resources needed elsewhere. Some policy-makers, however, maintained that more ambitious hopes could still be nourished, especially those like Colonel North with a particular personal loyalty to the men in the field. So, as was apparent in the hearings of 1987, the enterprise of keeping the Contras more or less in action, despite Congress's denial of funds through the Boland amendments, grew like some monstrous tropical vine in the White House basement, reaching out air-roots to draw financial nourishment from such surprising sources as the Sultan of Brunei and the King of Saudi Arabia, as well as the profits from the arms-transfers to Iran.

The actual underlying rationale for a degree of Administration concern with the small states of Central America which many observers (especially those outside the US) thought excessive was not often expatiated upon by official spokesmen, because it raised issues of great diplomatic delicacy with a sensitive neighbour. The preoccupation with the smaller states was for some policy-makers an indirect side effect of (or a figleaf for) anxiety about Mexico. Washington's relations with its immediate southern neighbour are always necessarily and inevitably beset by minefields of potentially explosive issues. There is the brooding Mexican memory of the nineteenth-century relationship, and an early twentieth-century relationship not much more comfortable. The highly permeable border had become a source of major social tensions in much of the American south-west, intrinsically tied into the out-of-control problems of immigration and the drug trade. Those tensions had their political impacts in Mr Reagan's Washington. They were accompanied by rising anxiety over an even more immediate source of possible instability in the relationship: the great burden of Mexican debt to foreign banks, especially the nine major US banks. Debt service (on about $100 billion of debt in the late years of the Reagan period) had tended to eat up most of Mexico's hard currency earnings, especially during the sharp fall in oil prices of the mid-1980s. The austerity programme that the government was obliged to impose to meet IMF prescriptions depressed the real standard of living. The political 'establishment' which had run the country for more than fifty years appeared to be under challenge from more radical forces, as was amply apparent in the 1988 elections. American efforts to combat the flow of drugs and 'undocumented' immigrants across the border were liable to produce sudden sharp crises in the always tense and complex relationship. The well-meaning Jimmy Carter had managed to grate considerably on Mexican sensitivities through some verbal infelicities: President Reagan likewise, through his choice of Ambassador.

The level of US concern with the southern border was indicated by the fact that Reagan as President-elect paid a visit to Mexico before his inauguration and found time for very regular meetings with the Mexican presidents in his years of office. In policy-making circles the view prevailed that if, in addition to the other factors making for an uncertain future for Mexican–American relations, there had to be added the problems which would be posed by a whole clutch of potential zealous leftist governments in Central America and the Caribbean, the prospects of maintaining the precarious co-operation would become still more dubious. And if, on a worst-case analysis, Mexico should swing out of the American orbit into that of the Soviet Union, as Cuba had done in the Eisenhower years, that development would undoubtedly represent the most catastrophic single injury to America's strategic circumstances since Pearl Harbor. It would force a reassessment of American ability to commit forces to maintain the balance in Europe, and create sentiment for a retreat to a 'Fortress America', thus perhaps damaging the American alliance system beyond repair. So the Washington preoccupation with Central America had a more complex (if somewhat paranoic) strategic basis than was usually conceded to it in Europe, and one which in the worst case would be totally disruptive to Europe's own security.

The most urgent visible crisis during the initial years of the Reagan period, however, was over El Salvador, where the left-wing insurgents had hopefully announced their 'final offensive' against the then government just before the Reagan inauguration. President Carter had become so concerned at the prospects that he enacted military aid into law only five days before he left office. El Salvador went on looking like the next feasible gain for the communist bridgehead in Central America for more or less the whole of the Reagan period and in the early Bush months. The Christian Democrat centre government of José Napoleón Duarte appeared for a time in 1985–6 to have established at least a temporary viability against challenges both from the left-wing insurgents and from right-wing 'death squads' who represented as real a danger and did more damage to the reputation of the government in the outside world. But by the end of the Reagan years both the far right and the far left appeared to have undermined the precarious hold of the political centre on power and territory. The reasons for the see-sawing balance seem to have included US support for the El Salvador armed forces, and the political and economic limitations (and later illness) of President Duarte. US aid, for instance, had enabled the army to be doubled to about 50 000 men supported by ground attack jets, attack helicopters, troop-carrying helicopters and Honduras-based American reconnaissance aircraft to monitor the movements of the guerrillas. The flow of military aid to the insurgents (through Nicaragua from Cuban sources) could not match that, but the obstacles to real economic and social progress vitiated the Duarte government's appeal.

In the Caribbean, contrasted techniques of overt and covert intervention were used to dispose respectively of a murderous but shaky Marxist faction which had seized power in Grenada, and the still more murderous but much longer-established hereditary autocracy which had held power for many years in Haiti. Grenada is so small an entity as a sovereign state that the successful American invasion (or 'rescue mission' as the Administration preferred to call it) may, in terms of the analysis I have been proposing, be regarded primarily as a declaratory signal, the declaration in effect being that there were firm limits to Washington's tolerance of erratic political radicalism in the Caribbean. In that sense, it was a gesture intended for more substantial audiences than the under-100 000 people of the island itself. One of the audiences was domestic: the US public, at a bad moment in Lebanon, was undoubtedly much cheered (indeed excessively so[34]) by the success of the operation, and it caused no problems, save a minor temporary glitch in President Reagan's relations with the most loyal (on all other issues) of his allies, Margaret Thatcher. When the coup attempt was made, since Grenada was a Commonwealth country, the call for help from the Governor as Head of State ought, constitutionally speaking, to have gone to London rather than Washington. But the Governor, as the man on the spot, seems to have assumed (no doubt rightly) that action from Washington would be faster and more certain, given that there were a large number of American students on the island whose safety could provide a rationale for the operation. (On the account given by Tip O'Neill, no one even remembered to notify Margaret Thatcher until he pointed out that Grenada was a member of the Commonwealth.) The airfield which the Cubans had been constructing and which had been described by Washington spokesmen as a security danger before the invasion, was later completed by a British company under American supervision and reclassified as a tourist facility, and thus a major asset in the islanders' hopes for a more prosperous future.

The other Caribbean operation, the winding-up of the Duvalier family autocracy on Haiti, evoked initially fewer doubts, the only complaints being that it had been delayed so long. Officially, Washington seems to have lost patience only about December 1984, but the regime had for decades been universally regarded as among the most disgraceful in the Western hemisphere, exploiting a bitterly-poor peasantry for the benefit only of the ruling family and their immediate coterie, through the use of a particularly brutal system of repression by secret police (the 'ton-ton macoute'). The longer-term results of the Duvaliers' departure remained highly uncertain. Few signs of economic reform or political stability had developed by 1988: the elections, when finally held, were dubious, and the prospect seemed to be emerging of another 'strong man' regime. Inevitably a good many setbacks of that sort had to be expected in the struggle for democracy in Latin America and the Caribbean, even in societies much more economically substantial than Haiti.

South Africa represented much the same sort of problem for US policy-makers as did many Third World societies: an unrepresentative oligarchy successfully excluding a large majority of the population from political power and (despite standards of development superior to most of Africa) excluding them from a fair share of the national economic cake as well. But in the South African case there were also two very important extra dimensions to the problem. The oligarchy (about 15 per cent of the population) which ran the society was white and the remaining 85 per cent black or brown; and the oligarchy was strongly entrenched and long-established. Moreover, the South African economy had become the powerhouse of economic life for Southern Africa as a whole. It was able to maintain relatively efficient armed forces by local standards, and had quite possibly even developed the capacity to make nuclear weapons as well as advanced military aircraft and other substantial strategic assets. So the assumption had to be made that the regime would be no pushover for even a well-developed internal insurgency. It could undoubtedly mount punitive strikes against its immediate neighbours almost at will, and by imposing severe economic disabilities on them, by way of reprisals, even bring some of them to disaster. It held further potential bargaining chips in the form of ability to withhold supplies of scarce strategic minerals (chrome, manganese, platinum) of great importance to the Western powers for military as well as civilian uses. It possessed a long sea-coast, very difficult to blockade and potentially of strategic importance in the protection of or attack on oil routes from the Persian Gulf (many tankers being too large for the Suez Canal). In the event of major crisis, the Cape route from the Atlantic to the Indian and Pacific Oceans might be the only one available, the Mediterranean being too vulnerable.

Given that the regime in South Africa possessed these considerable strategic and diplomatic assets, the task of persuading the white minority to share power with the black majority was, until the Carter years, one with which most earlier American Administrations had been chary of involving themselves, especially as they had been under little domestic or international pressure to do so. In the early Reagan years, that seemed again to be more or less the case. The dramas consequent on the collapse of Portuguese power in Africa in the mid-1970s had been temporarily played out. Angola and Mozambique had Marxist governments but with plenty of problems on their hands. Political evolution had also moved on a notch in the former Southern Rhodesia, by then Zimbabwe, relatively stable and economically productive but heading towards mutation into a one-party state with a Marxist chief decision-maker, Robert Mugabe. The most urgent piece of unfinished business seemed at the time to be the status of Namibia, along with the faint hope of squeezing the Cubans out of Angola.

In these circumstances the Reagan Administration opted for a slow-motion strategy known as 'constructive engagement' whose priorities were to secure the American objectives in Namibia and Angola, while gradually nudging along the processes of change in South Africa itself, by very mild economic and diplomatic incentives.[35] 'Constructive engagement' and the election of Ronald Reagan were initially regarded with hopeful enthusiasm by the government in Pretoria. They were seen to represent an about-turn from the policies of the Carter Administration which, by the end of its time in office, had come to be viewed in South Africa as a more dangerous enemy than the Soviet Union, and as bent on the immediate destruction of South African society. That was not really surprising, given that Walter Mondale in 1977 in a confrontation with the then Prime Minister, John Vorster, had suggested 'one man, one vote' as a solution for South African problems. From an Afrikaner point of view, that implied the end of South African society as they hoped to preserve it. American policy at the UN had also appeared to the Afrikaners to be made by other dedicated enemies of their ideology, such as black Americans like Andrew Young and Donald McHenry.

By contrast, Mr Reagan himself seemed to retain an image of South Africa considerably at odds with historical and contemporary realities. In an interview early in his term he called it 'a country that has stood beside us in every war we've ever fought', though actually the Afrikaner political élite which now runs the country had during the Second World War been distinctly pro-Nazi. And in August 1985, again in an interview, he implied that segregation in South Africa had been eliminated, more or less as in the United States. In fact, the legal, institutional and social restrictions on black rights in South Africa remained greater than they had been in the US almost a century earlier.

So the declaratory signals in the early Reagan years, in the form of the President's own statements plus the choice of Chester Crocker as the chief policy-maker for the area, and the strategy spelled out in his much-quoted article, had originally seemed to indicate a spell of relatively mild American pressures, if any, for the policy-makers in Pretoria from those in Washington. But in fact, by the late Reagan years these assumptions had proved mistaken in every respect. The Secretary of State was meeting Mr Oliver Tambo of the African National Congress, an organization candidly dedicated to the overthrow of the South African regime, by armed force if necessary, and so one which might on the original declaratory signals of the Administration have been classed as a terrorist group rather than as freedom-fighters, especially as their best-known strategist, Joe Slovo, was a veteran Communist. Moreover, many of the biggest and most influential US firms (Coca-Cola, General Motors, IBM, Kodak) had decided to pull out of or sell their South African operations and once this trend became clear, other firms (including non-American ones like Barclay's Bank) tended to decide that at long last the writing was really on the wall, and departed likewise. Thus, in fact, US business began leading the general process of disinvestment in South Africa. Late in 1985 the President suffered one of his most conclusive foreign policy defeats – almost the only one up to 'Irancontragate' – when Congress overrode his veto on sanctions against South Africa. And also Mr Reagan had appointed a black American diplomat as US Ambassador in South Africa, a choice which originally was dismissed as a piece of 'tokenism', but which in fact appeared by 1987 to be securing a new channel of communication with the alternative black leadership in South Africa.

Furthermore, the UNITA rebels in Angola, led by Dr Savimbi and supported by South African military muscle as well as US weaponry, appeared to be having enough success at least to induce the Angola government to agree a deal for the departure of the Cubans. So all in all, the level of change in Southern Africa as a whole appeared by 1988 to be considerably greater than the critics of 'constructive engagement' had expected. The direction of change was ambivalent, in that militarily and economically the ruling Afrikaner élite appeared to be, in consequence, domestically challenged on the far right by conservatives even more obdurate against change. Yet the pressures of international feeling, and economic forces, also seemed stronger than ever, and much of the mutation was in the Reagan years.

Paradoxically again, as far as US domestic political feeling was concerned, the change in attitudes seemed to be rooted in reaction to the second Reagan electoral victory. The anti-apartheid groups in the US, especially the Transafrica group led by Randall Robinson, saw that victory as necessitating a strong new push to alter US policies on South Africa. The Democrats thus became more conscious of the importance of the black constituency (led by Jesse Jackson) to their own party's strength in Congress and to its hopes for 1988. Vulnerable Republicans in the Senate, especially in 1986, took the point that their party in turn might prove historically to be on the losing side with domestic constituencies as well as in South Africa itself. And, of course, the South African regime by its own barbarous treatment, especially of schoolchildren, made its continued tenure of power indefensible. The most surprising thing about all this was that Reagan policies which had originally appeared set in concrete proved to be so astonishingly fragile as soon as a moderately well-concerted blow was struck against them: rather like that 'breakaway' furniture used in films, a solid image camouflaging an essential lack of substance.

To return to the general question of the 'Reagan Doctrine', it seems in retrospect chiefly a banner under which established (rather pragmatic) operational policies (the existing supply of arms and funds by covert means to assorted Third World insurgencies, as in

Afghanistan and Angola) were 'hyped' by some journalists, bureaucrats and ideologists into an ambitious declaratory policy which could be endowed with the President's name. That declaratory construct was then proposed as the basis for larger operational policies to match it. But such successes as it seems to have achieved had very little indeed to do with the President himself, being the work primarily of policy-makers in Washington at about the level of Assistant Secretary or Under-secretary. One of the unnoticed effects (until the Iran arms imbroglio) of the highly dispersed style of decision-making in the Reagan administration was to allow an astonishing level of independent action – for good or ill – to relatively junior officials. The 'Reagan Doctrine' appears one of the examples of that process. What was actually done (most importantly in the supply of weapons like the Stinger missile) could very easily have been done in the name simply of *realpolitik*. Endowing it with ideological overtones about the pursuit of American democratic values was unconvincing to anyone even moderately acquainted with the national or tribal value-systems of the guerrillas in Afghanistan or Angola or Kampuchea. But it had the paradoxical benefit (or cost, according to one's point of view) of helping undermine right-wing authoritarian regimes, as well as the left-wing totalitarian ones against which it was primarily devised. Thus, if the Reagan policies towards the Third World had not been so dominated by concern over events in Nicaragua, they might well have been more popular with liberals oriented to the Third World than with neo-conservatives. American weapons-supply in the name of the Reagan Doctrine has certainly to be seen as an important factor of guerrilla success in Afghanistan, and an example which would perhaps induce hesitation about future great-power interventions in the Third World. No doubt the Soviet tendency to withdrawal, which seemed enshrined in a number of Mr Gorbachev's policies, had its origins mostly in domestic economic problems. But the decisions taken in Washington clearly influenced Soviet assessments of costs and risks in directions likely to induce restraint.

Unfortunately, it remained Central America, especially Nicaragua and El Salvador, and in the final months Panama, which did most to create the world's image of the administration's policies. And in those three countries the policies seemed damning: devious and intransigent, yet ineffective. Washington's policy-makers did not succeed in bringing down the Sandinistas, but the effort to do so cost them valuable moral and diplomatic capital. They did not succeed in sustaining the Contras as a viable alternative government, though the effort to do so cost them a painful domestic crisis. They did not manage in El Salvador to keep the democratic centre viable: it lost strength to both the left and the right. Even the apparently minor task of removing a discredited drug-dealing 'strong man' in Panama proved a source of embarrassment, particularly during the electoral debates. Those whose mental picture of Washington policy-makers attributes to them a sinister capacity to make their will effective all over the world would have reason to revise their assumptions on a study of Central America. Of all the areas of US foreign policy, it was the one which provided the best case against the administration, as George Bush sought and won the Presidency. Whether he could improve the record remained an open question, but the prospects in early 1989 seemed hopeful at least on Nicaragua.

On the larger issue of whether the 'Reagan Doctrine' changed the odds very substantially for guerrillas or resistance movements fighting the occupying forces of a superpower, as in Afghanistan, one might say that the military equipment supplied in the name of that doctrine, especially the 'Stinger' missile, does seem to have partially cancelled out the Soviet advantage in air-cover and air-supply. But the strategic lessons of Afghanistan and Angola may take as long to digest as those of Vietnam.

7. Trouble with Allies

Every style of diplomacy has costs, and throughout the Reagan years the President's characteristic style seemed to impose some of its heaviest costs in America's alliance relationships. That was manifested most audibly in loud grumblings among the NATO allies, but in less overt forms it was equally present elsewhere. The most visible impact on formal alliance structures involved, of all improbable places, New Zealand. More consequential true damage, however, was undoubtedly created among the informal US quasi-alliances of the Middle East. If, as I have argued earlier, the Reagan declaratory signals had some useful effects *vis-à-vis* the chief adversary power, one must balance those benefits against damage elsewhere. Unfortunately, in diplomacy by megaphone one cannot avoid reaching audiences other than the one intended. But it may, of course, nevertheless on balance still be justifiable as a calculated risk.

The Reagan Administration was initially received among America's European allies with a blast of what must be called pre-emptive disapproval. In fact, the newcomers got a worse 'opening press' than any other set of just-installed Washington policy-makers since the time of Mr Dulles. This was not a matter of allergic reaction to the President himself. He tended to be rather condescendingly accepted as an amiable figurehead, a congenial enough character who had a professional 'showbiz' way with a 'one-liner', but not much else on the ball. He did not arouse anything as sharp as the personal animosity which had existed between Helmut Schmidt and Jimmy Carter. Rather, the trouble was an over-estimate of the influence of neo-conservative doctrine on the actual policies of the new administration. It created an initial distrust or apprehension which fed into and magnified all the many subsequent frictions. The fact that the other chief NATO decision-makers during the Reagan years were themselves sturdily conservative, especially in their views of the Soviet Union, did nothing to reduce these frictions and apprehensions. As was pointed out earlier, some quite profound philosophical and intellectual differences exist on international politics between neo-conservatives and traditionalist conservatives, such as tended to be running the foreign policy establishments of all the West European states, even those (like France, Spain or Greece) in which the governments in power for part of the Reagan period were nominally leftist, or (as in the Nordic countries) of a generally left-liberal complexion.

The underlying component of American neo-conservatism which created this European reaction was one that might be classed as emotional rather than intellectual: its strand of more-than-averagely-assertive American nationalism. Nationalist feeling is, of course, universal but, like some wines, it does not travel well; so any national vintage, whether American or European, is always less palatable to outsiders when exported: a trifle jarring to their tastes and sensibilities. Moreover, the Europeans saw the Reagan vintage of American nationalism as carrying the danger of spilling over into American unilateralism. That dismaying possibility was demonstrated in European eyes by what was seen as Washington's pursuit of obsessive American preoccupations concerning, for instance, Central America or the Caribbean or Libya at the expense of the Alliance's interest in general stability *vis-à-vis* the Russians and reasonably equable relations with the Third World. A striking illustration of this kind of reaction was the fact that the only serious row between President Reagan and the most constant and wholehearted of his allies, Margaret Thatcher, was over his most successful piece of American unilateralism, the invasion of Grenada.

What irritated European conservatives in particular about neo-conservative assumptions, however, was the stress given to the alleged dangers in Europe of 'Finlandization'. Despite the Finns' own fervent rejection of both the word and the idea, the concept had come widely to be used among analysts of international politics (including liberal and left analysts) as a necessary piece of shorthand for conveying the situation of a government obliged to acquiesce in control from Moscow of its basic external policies, because it lacks the physical capacity to resist that control. Though geography has disobligingly placed them hard up against the sphere of Soviet power, the Finns (a high-spirited people though few in number) deny vehemently that they have been reduced to any such condition.[36] However, there is no precise equivalent for the word or its meaning in current diplomatic argument so they are probably stuck with it, unjust as it may be.

If the 'Finlandization', in the neo-conservative sense, of Finland itself was denied by the people most concerned, the allegedly probable equivalent fate for Western Europe was still more vehemently dismissed. West European diplomatic establishments have a long history of dealings with the political élites which have been in power in Moscow at various times and no high opinion of Russian skills, either in the Soviet period or the several previous centuries of which they have historical memories and archival records, dating back to the time of Ivan the Terrible's wooing of Elizabeth I of England. Implications from America that they were likely to lose their national shirts if they cultivated diplomatic and economic relations with the current crop of policy-makers in the Kremlin therefore tended to evoke snorts of rage – at the Americans not the Russians. So it was not precisely good for NATO atmospherics.

On the other hand, the appointment of Alexander Haig as Reagan's first Secretary of State soothed most of the worst initial apprehensions as far as West European policy-makers were concerned. His success in his NATO role had been considerable and he was already a familiar figure from his time with Dr Kissinger. His strategic and diplomatic orientation was fully compatible with those of the European decision-makers he had to deal with, and it was assumed that he would become the dominant voice in Mr Reagan's ear on foreign policy matters. Unfortunately, the fragility of that assumption and the uncertainty of Haig's length of tenure became apparent to the Europeans almost as soon as it became apparent to the Secretary of State himself. By the third or fourth month of the Reagan first term, speculation in Europe was revolving round the question of whether it was Edwin Meese or Richard Allen or Caspar Weinberger who was most likely to edge him out from the dominant role in foreign policy-making. Haig did, of course, survive almost eighteen months in office and managed, from the point of view of America's allies, to achieve some useful things in that time. (Especially from Britain's point of view at the time of the Falklands crisis. Without Haig and Weinberger, the dominant voice in the President's ear might have been Jeane Kirkpatrick's with her orientation to Latin America. If her reported views had prevailed, NATO might have been plunged into its most disruptive crisis ever.) But Haig did not get his way on some other important questions of crisis-management, either *vis-à-vis* the Soviet Union or *vis-à-vis* the Middle East situation.

The first of those issues rather prophetically showed the President and his immediate White House entourage as even *less* orientated towards neo-conservative strategies than the Secretary of State. The question was whether and when the President would lift the grain embargo that Jimmy Carter had imposed on the Soviet Union after the invasion of Afghanistan. That he would do so was an election promise to Mid-western farmers, and it might therefore be construed as a matter of political honour that it should be done without undue delay. On the other hand, the decision to go ahead with the lifting of the ban in April 1981, at a time when the Soviet Union was clearly contemplating the enforcement yet again of its fiat in Eastern Europe (specifically Poland), was hardly calculated to make credible the conservative (as well as neo-conservative) commitment to challenge at least the more oppressive aspects of Soviet dominance in that part of the world. In particular, neo-conservatives were angered by Washington's failure to put the Polish government into default on its large debt to the West.

The two years from this Polish episode at the end of 1981 to the change of tactics signalled by the Reagan speech of January 1984 constituted a first prolonged nadir of relations between the Reagan Administration and European opinion, with particularly low points over the Siberian gas pipeline, the Lebanon events of 1982, the first 'Star Wars' speech of March 1983 and the Grenada invasion of October 1983, though in between these bad patches there were short-term upswings. The Williamsburg, Versailles and Bonn meetings, for instance, allowed the President's personal congeniality to help conquer his allies' misgivings about his Administration's policies. Moreover, the Reagan Administration and the European foreign policy establishments were together in the vital and prolonged fight for the deployment of intermediate-range US missiles in Europe (Pershings and cruises) to balance the updated Soviet missiles in Eastern Europe, the SS–20s. The basic decision on that policy (the 'two-track' decision of 1979) stemmed from a European initiative, chiefly Helmut Schmidt's, with general governmental backing elsewhere. But most of the political battles to stay on the track had to be fought in the first three Reagan years. The adversary for both the American administration and the European foreign policy establishments was critical or dissenting opinion within the NATO countries, embodied in the European peace movement which refused to be convinced of the wisdom of the original decision. For several years the deployment seemed a matter of touch-and-go, especially among the smaller northern allies, Holland and Denmark, where the peace movement was particularly strong. The pressure on the European policy-makers to retreat from their 1979 decision was very heavy, and if they had in fact given way, the neo-conservatives in Washington would have flourished such yielding as evidence that 'Finlandization' really was just around the corner for Europe. Unilateralism would have been encouraged in Washington: anti-American neutralism would have been triumphant in Europe, and the policy-makers in the Kremlin would have been strengthened in their hopes that the peace movement could be turned into a useful tool for the disrupting of NATO. But in fact none of that happened: the European governments stood firm by their decision, the weapons were deployed and the Russians changed their diplomatic strategy and began to make more serious gestures on arms control. So the episode has to be put down as ultimately a very fair and valid success for the Alliance. Some of Mr Reagan's declaratory signals, however, certainly did not help: for instance, the speech of 16 October 1981 implying there there could be a tactical nuclear exchange without all-out war. That may theoretically be true, but it was an injudicious moment to remind the Europeans of their most dreaded scenario: a nuclear war fought exclusively in Europe.

From time to time throughout the Reagan years the level of Reagan polemics against the Soviet Union seemed more than matched by the level of European intellectual polemics against President Reagan.[37] But whether NATO was seriously damaged by these exchanges (which were waged primarily in the intellectual media rather than between policy-makers or within grass-roots opinion) seems doubtful. NATO conduces so solidly to the respective national interests of its European members and is so well understood to do so by the foreign policy élites currently in power in those capitals (and even by most of their domestic political opposite numbers) that it takes a good deal more than harsh words in the controversy of the moment to really shake the alliance. And though European policy-makers often sharpen their considerable wits on American foreign policy moralism (whether of the liberal-left or the far-right varieties), on the whole most of them, despite their scoldings, probably saw more true danger in President Carter's uncertain Wilsonianism than in President Reagan's airy moral rhetoric about the 'evil empire'. Left-liberal critics (as against conservative policy-makers) would, of course, make the opposite judgement, and they tended to be strongly represented in the media in Europe (not as publishers but as editors or working journalists and their TV equivalents), so the media debate gave a rather slanted view of élite opinion.

It seems in the nature of things that powers with a very long tradition of running the society of states, as was the case for the major West European capitals, should feel that the relative newcomers in Washington, to whom the task had perforce now fallen, had a strong tendency to get their strategies wrong. That same long diplomatic experience, however, inhibited them from reacting in ways likely to put the alliance into true jeopardy. They have tended, when a particular Administration's policies are judged unpalatable, to grit their teeth, set up a delaying manoeuvre, and hope that the next President to come along would see things differently. In all that there was not much difference between the Europeans' reactions to the Reagan Administration and their reaction to some of his predecessors. Kennedy was the only recent President whom the Europeans readily took to their hearts during his first years of office: admiration for others, like Truman and Eisenhower, was late and grudging. (Which probably goes to show that images are just as important in European popular judgements as in American, though the taste in them is rather different on the two sides of the Atlantic.)

Nevertheless, underlying the endemic frictions between Washington and the European capitals during the Reagan years (none of which, as far as present retrospect goes, constituted as real a clash of national interests as Suez in 1956, or produced as much true moral division as Vietnam) there was an additional factor that has to be rated as serious: the inescapable generation change and the inevitable readjustments that come with it. NATO was almost forty years old by Mr Reagan's last year of office. He belonged in actual age-cohort to the generation which put the bond together from both sides of the Atlantic (in 1948–9, during the first trauma of European and American adjustment to the idea that Soviet power presented a deadly danger to all pluralist societies), though he personally was, of course, otherwise engaged at the time. The younger rising politician or policy-maker by his time as President had no personal memory of the circumstances that brought this transatlantic connection into being. The consensus among the original foreign policy élite which created it had been shattered by Vietnam. A new bipartisan consensus on foreign policy may perhaps have been emerging during the Reagan years, but it will be some time before its durability can be established. Moreover, the foreign policy élite has itself changed. It used to be almost entirely white, Anglo-Saxon, male, mostly Protestant, mostly Eastern Establishment, mostly Ivy League. There was not an Ivy League President between Kennedy and the present incumbent: Johnson, Nixon, Ford, Carter and Reagan represented much more the ethos of small towns in the west and south than the Europe-orientated internationalist-minded élites of the East Coast. The direction of major economic connections has also changed: the Pacific basin, especially of course Japan, has provided the predominant focus for some years in economic-future calculations. The population distribution within the US has changed with more of the citizenry (and therefore more electoral clout) moving to the 'Sunbelt' and the West. The racial mix of the US population has changed and will change still faster over the next few decades, since most new immigration is now from Latin America or from Asia. So the newly-arrived East European 'ethnics' who used to have so large an impact on American foreign policy will be replaced by others. Not since the Berlin crises of 1958–61 had Europe generated a level of superpower conflict that seemed high enough to carry a risk of war. Tensions that last found dramatic expression thirty years ago were bound to appear dim and remote to younger people. So the general reasons why there were still more than 300 000 US troops in Europe, apparently defending a continent whose indigenous defenders, the West Europeans, were more numerous (320 million) than US citizens, about as rich, almost as technologically sophisticated, and with long, strong, redoubtable military traditions and experience of their own, were naturally not exactly clear to the average American voter. Indeed the situation had come to seem pretty indefensible even to some very sophisticated analysts of the Alliance's affairs, like Dr Kissinger, Dr Brzezinski or Senator Sam Nunn. The conventional Alliance answer, that the US troops are in Europe not for the defence of Europe but as the forward defence line of the United States itself, may be strategically sound but raises some awkward political questions. The alternative valid answer, that they are there because that is the arrangement which has been found to keep the balance of power stable and the chance of Soviet adventurism in Europe low, may provide an adequate reason but is much more convincing to those able to remember the past than to those who do not. The 1984 Nunn amendment (which in effect threatened to take the US troops out of Europe unless the Europeans were a bit less slack about financing an adequate defence for themselves) may be considered the Reagan-era version of a strategic irritation that has been endemic in the Alliance for more than thirty years now.

These factors, which made the Atlantic bond sometimes seem more fragile during the Reagan years then it had been earlier, had obviously been developing since well before his time, and would probably have been still more visible by the early 1980s if Jimmy Carter had got a second term. However, one factor in the frictions undoubtedly stemmed from the most characteristic early Reagan diplomatic technique: his strong declaratory signals. (Some British bystanders were given to adapting to them Wellington's comment on his own troops: 'I don't know if they frighten the enemy, but by God they terrify me.') The style of signalling represented, for instance, by the Reagan speech of 16 October 1981 on tactical nuclear exchange without all-out war, or by Haig's speech a week or two later on a possible nuclear 'warning explosion', along with some of the speeches by Weinberger and assorted American generals or admirals on 'warfighting' capacity as against deterrence, or the potential implications of the 'air–land' battle doctrine being developed in NATO, with the 'follow-on-forces attack' (FOFA) strategy, or the maritime strategic doctrine: all these could be seen by hard-pressed European policy-makers as playing into the hands of dissenting opinion and the peace movements in their respective countries, by raising the level of nuclear anxiety and thus increasing the difficulties of maintaining course on the 'two-tracks' decision.

A strong component of nationalist feeling must be noted in the attitudes of the European allies on nuclear weapons and nuclear doctrine. Evidence of this may be seen in that France, where the nuclear weapons are entirely French and French decision-makers' fingers are on the nuclear triggers, was largely untouched by the anti-nuclear movement. Britain, where there are US bases and the weapons-system is part-American, was periodically subject to waves of 'grassroots' feeling that seemed in equal parts anti-nuclear and anti-American. The defence policy of the British Labour Party in opposition seemed originally to indicate that if it had achieved office in 1987 (which of course it did not), there would be a major NATO crisis in Mr Reagan's last year. The result of the election postponed that possibility to 1992, and the obvious rejection by the electorate of Labour's defence policy eventually forced Neil Kinnock to change it, but similar electoral potentialities exist in the smaller European countries.

In the later Reagan years, a fear also developed in the European NATO countries that if the SDI came to anything much, it might lead to a 'decoupling' of American security from the defence of Europe, since the US might be safe (or believe itself to be safe) inside a new 'high-tech' version of 'fortress America'. Defending Europe without American help would be difficult, though not impossible, for the West Europeans. It would mean, for instance, finding five more divisions of combat troops to replace the Americans taken out of the line, plus extra air force and navy equivalents for the US forces now stationed in the NATO area. Over the long term, that would probably mean a doubling of the proportion of European GNP spent on defence, from the present 3–4 per cent (higher in Britain) to 5–6 per cent, which would put it on the same level as the US seems likely to be. However, even such an increased sacrifice of resources would by no means necessarily maintain the stability of the past forty years in the central-power balance, since that stability has depended essentially on the clear signal, to the adversary decision-makers in Moscow, that the US would be involved from the very first day of any attack in Europe, since American troops were visibly deployed across the essential invasion routes. Thus, so long as the deterring of Soviet expansion of its power-sphere in Europe remained a common interest of Washington and the West European capitals, the case for at least some US deployments in Europe remained basically solid. The argument that US funds would be saved by taking the troops back home was quite fallacious, unless it was also assumed that they would be demobilized. Rehousing them at home plus building logistic capacity to get them back to Europe when needed would, in fact, mean substantially increased costs. But for those who had not personally observed the consolidation of Soviet power over Eastern and Central Europe in the 1940s, these arguments were difficult to make convincing.

Finally, there was the point that NATO's earlier decades were mostly decades of relatively continuous economic growth for the Western economies as a whole, even though some countries were less successful than others and occasional phases of recession developed (as, for instance, in the first two Reagan years and as appeared threatened after the end of his second term). Given the predicted faltering of world economic growth in the early 1990s, the question had to be faced of whether an alliance structure constructed in boom times could survive in a less favourable world economic climate, such as seemed possibly to be foreseeable especially during the penultimate Reagan year, about the time of the Wall Street crash. The level of economic argument across the Atlantic – over steel, or the Common Agricultural Policy, or protectionism, or the high American interest rates that at one stage were draining off capital from Europe – seemed never less than strident, even before then.

Both the economic arguments with Europe and the nuclear anxieties there had close parallels in Japan. In some ways the trans-Pacific alliance with Japan could be held to be a more fragile and artificial arrangement than the trans-Atlantic alliance with Western Europe. The peoples involved did not stem from the same blend of cultures or share the same kind of background assumptions and traditions. Japan was a defeated enemy, not an historic ally, in the early postwar period when it was recruited to the US coalition. Moreover, Japan managed subsequently to prosper beyond the wildest dreams of its people on the basis of access to American markets and initially-American technology. The economic consequences of that phenomenal competitive success of the society that had been recreated under US protection were, by the Reagan years, exceedingly bitter for many Americans. Protectionist reactions specifically against Japan had become very strong in the US by the mid-1980s, and though the Reagan administration worked hard and, for most of the time, successfully at reducing their potential impact, they remained a permanently ticking time-bomb within the Japanese–American relationship, especially after the Republicans lost control of the Senate in 1986.

On nuclear and strategic matters, likewise, the differences between American and Japanese opinion seemed at about the same level as that between American and European opinion. The Europeans had, it was true, a stronger anti-nuclear movement; but there was no precise European equivalent of the 'Three Non-Nuclear Principles', to which every Japanese government must pay at least plausible lip-service ('Not possessing nuclear weapons: not producing nuclear weapons: not permitting their introduction into the country'). It was the third of the three principles which created potential difficulties for American strategists, since US ships had a need to visit Japanese ports, and a very substantial proportion of those ships, by the Reagan years, were nuclear-armed. In fact, the difficulty continued to be overcome by a Nelson-like policy on the part of successive Japanese decision-makers of clapping the telescope to the blind eye when a US naval ship was in port and failing to see any signal that it was nuclear-armed. That is, they adopted an unspoken convention that the temporary presence in Japanese ports (or territorial waters or air-space) of American nuclear weapons would not be construed as violation of the injunction against introduction of nuclear weapons into Japan. That arrangement still appeared likely to continue workable at the end of the Reagan years, since the Liberal Democratic Party remained in power (even increasing its already substantial majority in 1986) and also continued to maintain a consensus in its favour. But there appeared to be a delicate asymmetrical balance between American tolerance of a level of Japanese imports that many Americans resented, and Japanese tolerance of American nuclear ship visits that quite a few Japanese resented. So American protectionist feeling directed against Japan, often forcefully expressed in Congress, represented a threat to the linchpin of American strategic interests in the Pacific.

The most surprising formal alliance crisis of the Reagan years was the one involving New Zealand and Australia. Yet in fact, this little episode of alliance crisis-management illustrated very neatly the Administration's basic technique of making a declaratory signal 'stand-in' for more substantial measures. New Zealand had since 1951 been a member of the ANZUS alliance (Australia–New

Zealand–US), a treaty which until 1984 had hardly ever furrowed the brows of Americans (even the handful of State Department specialists who dealt with its affairs) in the entire 33 years of its existence. But New Zealanders shared the kinds of nuclear anxieties which had grown in British opinion, and from time to time they elect a Labour government. (The New Zealand Labour Party stems from a Social Democratic political movement and has a good deal in common with the British Labour Party.) From about 1966 nuclear anxiety within the NZ Labour movement was strong enough to constitute heavy pressure on any potential Labour Prime Minister to refuse port visits by nuclear-armed, nuclear-powered or even nuclear-capable ships. In the normal course of events, the only such ships likely to want to visit New Zealand ports would, of course, be US naval ships, so the pressure for a ban represented a theoretical problem for CINCPAC. But only a theoretical problem for, unlike Japan, New Zealand is a very long way from any potential theatre of engagement and there is no serious operational requirement to deploy ships in or out of its ports. There had been, in fact, a Labour government in New Zealand between 1972 and 1975, and the Prime Ministers of that time reportedly asked Washington not to send nuclear-powered or nuclear-armed ships. The request seems to have been accepted with a shrug by the Washington policy-makers of the time (President Nixon and Dr Kissinger, who certainly had more urgent questions on their agenda), and it was given no great publicity. Whether the injunction was interpreted so as to prevent visits also by nuclear-*capable* ships is a moot point: some New Zealand analysts say there were such visits during that period. But no US reprisals were proposed which would disturb the routine working of the alliance. Labour lost office in 1975 and the question thus disappeared for almost ten years. By the time another Labour Prime Minister, David Lange, was returned to office (July 1984) the question had acquired more salience with New Zealand opinion. Various developments during the intervening years, especially French testing of nuclear weapons in the Pacific, had exacerbated a sort of general nuclear resentment and created stronger pressure from the left of the party on the Prime Minister to take a high-profile stand against ship visits. So he duly announced his stand. But Washington, instead of again shrugging the matter off as of no operational importance (as had been done earlier) and waiting for a change in government, decided to take a stand of its own on alliance principle. As a Reagan official put it: 'Unless we hold our allies' feet to the fire over ship visits and nuclear deployments, one will run away and then the next. . . . We will not be put in a position where they want our protection but without the necessary weapons in place to do the job.'

In other words, the New Zealand case was interpreted as a good moment for a declaratory signal to the American alliance system as a whole – about forty countries in various parts of the world – that alliances are a two-way street: the minor power as well as the major power undertakes strategic obligations. And if the major power's global strategy is based on nuclear-strike capacity, that essentially means becoming part of a nuclear strategy. In effect, the New Zealand government sought to deny that strategic and political implication: to have its non-nuclear cake and eat it in the security of an alliance with a nuclear power. New Zealand did not seek to leave the alliance and there is no provision in the treaty for any member to be *de jure* expelled. Nor did the Prime Minister argue that other countries should follow the NZ example. He simply wanted to have it both ways for his own society. Washington in reply signalled loud and clear the diplomatic equivalent of 'no way'. So New Zealand was explicitly reduced from the status of an ally to that of a friend, which meant no treaty consultations, no access to US-originated intelligence, no joint exercises, no special access to advanced technology, no special pleading by the State Department if NZ exports were targeted by protectionist forces in the US Congress. Thus in effect, NZ was 'made an example of', sending a declaratory signal to other, far more vital, American allies like, for instance, Britain, whose Labour Party was obviously tempted to assume (along perhaps with Norway or Denmark or the Netherlands) that they too could make a bid for a 'free ride': the advantages of alliance with a superpower without any costs. On the whole one would say that the 'demonstration effect' probably worked: the far more vulnerable European powers were signalled the potential costs of following New Zealand into exile from the US alliance-structure. And, of course, if a superpower is wanting to use one of its allies for a demonstration effect, logic degrees choosing the most marginal of them. No country could have been more marginal to US security than New Zealand, so it was a logical choice, though a bit analogous to a schoolmaster choosing to make an example of the smallest boy in the class.

During the final phase of the Reagan presidency, from late 1986, all these earlier problems of the alliance relationships were entirely overlaid by the fallout from Reykjavik and 'Irancontragate', and the fears generated by the 1987 Wall Street crash. For the Europeans, Reykjavik was the more important in substance and in the implications which have been discussed in an earlier chapter. On Iran and the arms deal for the Contras, there was a certain 'we always knew it' glee in the tone of much European media comment. Mr Reagan's standing as a foreign policy-maker was so low at that time that any additional damage was rather in the class of just one extra dent in a much-battered car. For the Arab quasi-allies of the United States, certainly, the delivery of American arms to Iran was a major addition to their litany of grievances, and the apparent role of Israel in facilitating the whole deal a confirmation of their worst suspicions. But on the other hand, despite the general disgruntlement of the Arab countries with the Reagan administration, they still needed the help of Washington in fending off the dangers arising from the Iran–Iraq war. The smaller Arab countries of the Gulf had almost as much to fear from Iraq as from Iran, and the somewhat Machiavellian dealings in arms and intelligence brought to light by the Congressional enquiries and investigative journalism in Washington would not by any means have distressed them, if it had been clear that it helped prevent either side from securing a conclusive victory.

By the last Reagan year, the impact of decisions (or more probably, non-decisions) in Washington on the global economy preoccupied America's allies as much as anything in the direct foreign-policy field. The 1987 Wall Street crash had been widely blamed by European analysts on ill-considered remarks by James Baker during his arguments with West Germany's economic authorities over interest rates. But that issue rapidly became far less important than the question of whether Washington would, or even could, respond adequately to pressures for action to prevent the stockmarket crash from precipitating a recession, or even a depression, in 1990 or later. Allied decision-makers spoke up more loudly and boldly than they had ever previously ventured to do about the necessity to cut the US budget deficit: for instance, the British Prime Minister, Mrs Thatcher, in private messages to the

President, and her Chancellor of the Exchequer, Nigel Lawson, in public speeches,[38] along with many other allied heads of government.

The apprehension that a lame-duck President and a fractious, self-serving Congress in election year could, through delayed effects, bring the Western world to economic ruin became audible in normally sympathetic conservative quarters where it never previously would have been raised. The *Economist*, for instance, in its issue of November 7–13 1987 darkly contemplated a 'worst case' scenario in which a further fall of the dollar precipitated panic selling by foreign holders of US currency and said bluntly that the potential resulting catastrophe would be an 'economic equivalent of nuclear war', and that any such disaster must be attributed to the weaknesses of US political leadership. Thus, though towards the end of his years in office President Reagan no longer excited fears that he was determined on confrontation with the Soviet Union or that he was likely to launch into major combat operations in the Persian Gulf or Nicaragua, his economic policies had replaced his foreign policies as a source of apprehension and sometimes rage. But the success of the INF negotiations and the prospect of a possible further success for arms control on long-range strategic missiles as well did a great deal to redeem the reputation of his administration in the eyes of America's allies, even though they had some qualms about the eventual strategic impact of these changes.

8. 'All Smoke and Mirrors?'

'Sometimes our right hand doesn't know what our far-right hand is doing.' That was among President Reagan's 'one-liners' in the happy and lucky earlier years of his Presidency, but by 1987 the insouciance of the joke had come to seem damning rather than engaging. That is to say, his characteristic 'laid-back' and relaxed style had come to be defined, in the Tower Commission report and much of the subsequent comment, as the source of the weakness of control which had allowed the erratic and damaging operations of Colonel North and his colleagues to develop in the White House basement. Though that Reagan style had been in operation from the beginning, during the first term any resulting problems had apparently been camouflaged by the relatively strong team in the White House around the President. But in the second term, with that team dispersed and the President's own energy further sapped by age and ill-health, it came to appear a fundamental issue; a basic source of the uncertainties about the final assessments of his Presidency.

Obviously, some of the people inside the Administration had noted this phenomenon, even in the earliest period. Haig, for instance:

> To me the White House was as mysterious as a ghost ship: you heard the creak of the rigging and the groan of the timbers and sometimes even glimpsed the crew on deck. But which of the crew had the helm?[39]

David Stockman's account of the decision-making process provides an equally foggy picture, for instance, on the evolution of the defence budget. Aside from the unsurprising points that particular victories went to the shrewdest and sharpest players of the bureaucratic game (such as Weinberger) and that even Stockman had to concede the necessity of being 'guided by what was politically possible, not by what was doctrinally correct',[40] the locus of decision-making seemed equally uncertain to him. Obviously, it will be only with the passage of time, the publication of still more memoirs and the release of documents that it will be possible to see that aspect of the Reagan presidency in full perspective.

Meantime, from the viewpoint of this provisional and interim analysis, the foreign policy of the period looks (beneath the general intellectual incoherence) primarily like an object-lesson in the pitfalls (but in some respects, paradoxically, the advantages) of rhetoric. In the Iran imbroglio, for instance, if Mr Reagan had not so zealously talked a high moral line, especially about no dealings with terrorists, there would have been much less shock to US opinion in the disclosure of the actual dealings. In themselves, as operational policies, they might otherwise even have commanded a reasonable level of support. Getting hostages out of the hands of terrorists is in itself an objective that no one could quarrel with. And even the most ostentatiously tough-minded of other governments, despite their denials, had frequently provided 'ransoms' of various sorts. The Israelis, for instance, had tended to hand over large groups of young Arabs (potential soldiers or terrorists) to retrieve tiny numbers of captive Israeli soldiers or airmen (at last count, more than 6000 Arabs for nine Israelis).

The second main element in the deal (the effort to get on to better terms with any less unreasonable groups among the possible successors in Iran after Ayatollah Khomeini's death) had so much strategic and diplomatic logic to it, in the eyes of America's allies, that even though in Washington it was usually presented as a mere rationale or cover-story, to most non-American observers it appeared the best justification of the envisaged deal – provided, of course, that the potentially 'moderate' or at least pragmatic factions had been correctly identified (which seems very doubtful) and that the arms supplied were not in a quantity or of a quality to increase Iran's chance of victory (which on the final outcome seems probable). The third element – diversion of the profits (along with solicited contributions from assorted donors) to sustain the Contras during the period in which Congress had cut off funding – commanded practically no support abroad, since very few of America's allies regarded the bringing-down of the Sandinistas as either necessary, justifiable or feasible. On the other hand, that objective was not short of backers in the Republican ranks. By

March 1987, 52 per cent of the electorate were inclined to cut off funding to the Contras, but the hearings, especially Colonel North's testimony, operated paradoxically to improve their image. Presidents have not infrequently used surreptitious means to get round Congressional efforts to tie their hands in matters they regard as touching national security, so the revealed deviousness was not unprecedented enough to cause major trauma. Moreover, the Boland amendments, though having the force of law for a time, did not represent set-in-concrete sentiment even in Congress, which had again reversed itself and resumed the funding of the Contras by the time the hearings were under way.

One may argue, therefore, that the moral indignation generated over the Iran imbroglio derived less from the operational policies themselves (all their aspects having some apologists) than from the excessively blatant contrast between what had earlier been said and what was in due course revealed as having been done. That is, the contrast between the rhetoric and the *realpolitik*, the declaratory and the operational policy. The first was full of pious high-mindedness and assertive tough-mindedness. The second embodied a species of low-grade Machiavellianism, especially, for instance, in the apparent assassination attempt on Gaddafi, the projects for kidnappings, the apparent 'cooking' of intelligence data given to the two sides in the Iran–Iraq war, the hiking-up of prices for the arms and the use of disreputable middle-men.

It therefore seems reasonable to define the situation, as was argued earlier, as one in which Presidential credibility fell, at least for a time, into the gaping chasm between the operational and the declaratory policy. But equally one has to say that the damage derived primarily from the declaratory policy, in that it generated false public expectations which could not over the long term be met. Moreover, once those expectations *had* been generated, the effort to fulfil them at least partially in turn generated the sort of operational policies which ended in a fiasco that damaged the Presidency in both domestic and foreign policy in a crucial late stage of its operations.

The reason why the Administration came to grief over the anti-terrorist campaign rather than over the many other aspects of foreign policy in which the same dichotomy had been observable (as this book has hoped to show) is that the man-in-the-street was rather more inclined and qualified to make a judgement in that particular field than in most others. Also the government of the Ayatollah was more resented and detested by the average man-in-the-street than even the Libyan government, since almost everyone could remember the long year of anguish over the hostages in Teheran and the nightly burnings of the American flag or Uncle Sam in effigy. The issue of hostages brought the complexities of international politics down to something like familiar domestic crime. Thus precisely the sort of person who was normally a Reagan loyalist and a strong 'law and order' man or woman would tend to be particularly shocked at payment of a ransom in arms to the Iranian regime in whose interests the terrorists acted. As someone said, it was like a John Wayne movie in which the hero ends up selling guns to the Indians.

There was a neat, macabre symbolism in the fact that the ancient Ayatollah in Iran was a source of grief for both Mr Carter and Mr Reagan, and their respective groups of ideological activists. He embodied in his person, his historic record and the situation of the country he controlled exactly those elements of Third World reality that American foreign policy-makers (both the liberals round Mr Carter and the neo-conservatives round Mr Reagan) found most difficult to fit into their systems of assumptions. Much more than Mr Gorbachev ever could, he symbolized the power of non-Western, non-predictable, non-rational elements in the society of states – a sort of grim old Rock of Ages on which two successive modern sophisticated Titanics (for despite their difficulties both administrations were that) were to damage themselves.

A common factor in the vulnerability of the two Administrations was built-in Utopianism: right-wing Utopianism in Mr Reagan's case, and left-liberal Utopianism in Mr Carter's. The characteristic that distinguishes Utopianism of either kind is a preoccupation with the world-as-it-should-be, the world as wish or aspiration, as against the world-as-it-is, which is the preoccupation of realism. The basic proposition of left-liberal Utopianism, as in Mr Carter's time, was the assumption that power relationships could and should be down-played as an element in international politics. Right-wing Utopianism by contrast tends to have a strong component of aggrieved nationalism: to look (as in some European cases) to restored imperial glory or, in the American case, to restoration of an imagined golden age of American invulnerability and therefore power. Mr Reagan's chosen version of SDI was a particularly neat symbolic example of that.

The more obvious differences in political philosophy between the two Presidents camouflaged for most people the points on which their stances were distinctly similar. Each initially presented and (as far as present evidence goes) apparently saw the conflicts of international politics largely in moral terms. Both originally implied that the moral assumptions of American foreign policy were not only important in themselves, but provided useful or even vital weapons in the American diplomatic armoury. (Brzezinski had made a good deal of that argument in his criticisms of the alleged lack of moral feeling in the Kissinger period.) Both propounded the notion of American 'exceptionalism': US society as the 'shining city on a hill', its values and mores a beacon for all the world.

In that assumption of American exceptionalism the neo-conservatives who adopted Mr Reagan as their political figurehead presented a kind of mirror-image of the liberals whose earlier influence on policy they tended to see as the source of the troubles of American foreign relations. For both groups saw the US as the 'last best hope of mankind', and that assumption can be held either to require higher US moral standards in foreign policy than had been characteristic of other great powers of the past, or alternatively, to justify indefinite amounts of skulduggery on the rationale of serving a cause vital and virtuous enough to warrant breaking the established rules. That latter position was, in fact, a Leninist one. 'The safety of the Revolution is the supreme law' had been the basis of Russian Communist Party decision-making since about 1902. And it transmuted very easily into 'the safety of the national interest is the supreme law'.

The proclamation that some chosen Utopia lies at the end of some particular road may, of course, be useful to effecting progress in a more mundane but quite desirable direction. A world free of power-politics, or free of nuclear weapons, or free of threats to the American national interest may be useful to offer as aspirations, even if they remain unlikely to be attained as objectives. Nevertheless, looking back over the past twelve years (the Carter and Reagan years) of American foreign policy one is bound to ask whether the respective ideological banners of both Presidents were not impediments rather than assets on the march, whether such capacity as they possessed to inspire the troops justified the extra burdens they imposed. Whether it might not have been better to 'elevate them sights a little lower', as one of the more successful Civil War generals once said. That is, whether American foreign policy might not have been more stable and coherent through the whole period if the assumptions that underlie it had defined America's role in the world less ambitiously, acknowledged the US as less autonomous, less able to mould the world to its own pattern or make the rules for the society of states, than it used to be: subject to much the same vulnerability and constrictions on policy-making as other past and present great powers in the society of states.

There was, however, another reason for some eventual similarities of embarrassment in the cases of two Presidencies infused with, in many ways, contrasted strategic and ideological views. All recent Administrations in Washington have had in essence the same two basic tasks in international politics. First, managing the adversary relationship with the Soviet Union so that it produces neither war nor a Soviet victory without war; and secondly, managing a set of relationships with the rest of the world which have inescapably become those of reduced US paramountcy. The second of those two tasks was always especially painful to American nationalist feelings such as were particularly dominant in the Reagan administration. But the underlying necessities were historically just as pressing in the Reagan years as in the Carter years: more so indeed in some respects. They arose from historical processes of economic and social change whose momentum was beyond the control of any set of political decision-makers in Washington.

The nature of the reasons for reduced US paramountcy may be illustrated by one very striking statistic. At the end of the Second World War, the US was the single great, undamaged, fully developed economy of the world, and it accounted for almost half of world production. Forty years on, in Mr Reagan's time in office, the US share of world production was shrinking towards 22 per cent and was inevitably fated to shrink further as a proportion of total world output. This was not primarily because of an actual fall in US production or productivity, though they did rise less rapidly than in some other economies. It was chiefly because production in the rest of the world had either revived (as in Europe and Japan) or developed, as in the Third World. So the overall change was by no means a matter for regret: if it had not happened, the world of the late twentieth century would have been a far poorer and more distressed place than it is. But managing a process of declining economic paramountcy offered, by the Reagan years, problems which would have been painful for any set of Washington decision-makers and were particularly so to those imbued with the optimistic nationalism of the Reagan ethos.

There were some clear economic successes. Inflation was reduced to a bearable level, though it again posed a prospective threat at the end of the Reagan period. The tax system was reformed in a manner which seemed beneficial to most individual taxpayers and total tax revenues rose, despite the cuts, from about $500 billion to over $900 billion. Welfare expenditure rose by about $180 billion. The real growth rate, which had been about 4.5 per cent in the 1950s, averaged in the vicinity of 3 per cent during the Reagan years as it had in the Carter years. Unemployment fell towards 5 per cent. Borrowing from or investment by the outside world, however, rose at such a rate that the US was transformed from the world's largest creditor to its largest debtor. The budget and trade deficits blew out embarrassingly, though the fall in the value of the dollar was reducing the trade deficit by the end of the period. The flood-tide of imports (and the consequent fears for American jobs) created so strong a tendency in Congress to throw up protectionist barriers that the most diplomatically vital of America's alliances, those with Western Europe and with Japan, appeared in some danger. The inflow of funds (from Japan, Western Europe and Latin America) solved some immediate problems but at the cost of a longer-term increase in vulnerability to external forces. So though as Mr Reagan prepared for his exit the US economy remained the most powerful in the world, the sort of absolute ascendancy that it had once possessed (in the early postwar period) was more conclusively lost than it had been at his inauguration. And with the reduction of economic ascendancy there was bound to be some loss of diplomatic paramountcy. Yet his luck held: in his final months the six-year economic boom was still sustained, despite the Wall Street crash of 1987.

So if Presidents Reagan and Carter had more in common than was usually admitted, they differed in one way that was more significant than it may seem: Jimmy Carter's luck had run out in less than three years, whereas Ronald Reagan's lasted almost unblemished for six and eventually revived after the disasters of late 1986–7. As Machiavelli remarks, fortune rules half our fates: the other half we make ourselves. Up until late 1986 Ronald Reagan, by comparison with his immediate predecessors, had seemed to have enlisted the goddess of fortune as his personal guardian angel. Unlike those who came to office in 1969, he had no disastrous war to wind up. Unlike Mr Carter, he was not borne into office on a wave of liberal guilt-feeling and loss of US self-confidence. On the contrary, he benefited both domestically and internationally by the swing of the pendulum back to the normal US mood of nationalist buoyancy. Moreover, the prolonged succession crisis in Moscow and the resulting Soviet immobilism for the first four years meant less formidable decision-makers, initially, in the adversary capital than Kennedy, Johnson, Nixon and Carter had faced. Gorbachev was obviously a more capable adversary (especially at 'PR'), but not one whose mind, at least during the Reagan period, was at all bent on adventures abroad or opportunity-seizing in the Brezhnev manner of 1975–9. After the exit from Afghanistan, Eastern Europe seemed likely to absorb as much Soviet energy as could be spared from events at home. The general stagnation of the economies of the East European communist world, the painful drain on economic resources imposed by the arms race with America, and even the great Chernobyl nuclear disaster of April 1986: all could be judged as having confirmed Soviet policy-makers in a prudent avoidance, for the time being, of crises or new commitments and thus an aversion to new foreign adventures for the duration of the Reagan years, and probably the early Bush years.

Indeed, Mr Gorbachev might be regarded in two ways as an aspect of Mr Reagan's luck as a policy-maker. For during the Reagan years his preoccupation with reforming the Soviet economic system (and if his control over the party could be maintained, possibly even modifying the political system) kept him orientated towards crisis-avoidance and arms control. But his reforms had not yet, by the end of the Reagan years, had enough influence on Soviet practices to make the Soviet Union more formidable as a society, either economically or ideologically. It did, of course, remain very formidable militarily, though relatively a bit less so *vis-à-vis* the US than it had been in the late Carter years.

The political trend of events in China also remained in a

favourable phase for the West during the Reagan years, reducing to zero the chances of conflict on a policy front where it had seemed very likely at the time of his first election. Deng Xiao-Ping's aged hand remained at the helm of China's affairs as long as Mr Reagan's remained at the helm of America's affairs, if that is the right way of describing the President's role in the policy-process.

It has to be regarded as an equally notable piece of luck that the most active conflicts of Mr Reagan's time involved very small societies, in terms of population. Libya, Nicaragua, Lebanon and Grenada put together could hardly raise between them as much population as Greater New York. If there have to be trouble-spots in the world, small may not be beautiful but it is at any rate relatively manageable.

The governments of America's major allies mostly remained in solidly conservative hands until the end of the Reagan years. OPEC was rendered almost toothless by the luck of an oil-glut for his entire time in office. Without the favourable trends of oil supplies from 1980 on, the Iran–Iraq war and the problems of the Gulf generally would have been much more acute issues for the European capitals and Japan, as well as Washington. As it was, only the occasionally envisaged nightmare of a possible victory for Teheran cropped up to bother Western decision-makers, at least till the final flare-up of naval confrontation in the Gulf before the cease-fire. Even then, the probability remained that oil prices would rise only slowly from their low point of the mid-1980s, that supply might remain in glut until the early 1990s, and that the needs of Iran and Iraq for funds for postwar reconstruction would strengthen that trend.

Those who were outraged at the Reagan Administration's visibly increasing reliance on pragmatism as a guiding principle in foreign policy were mostly on the far right, wanting a larger quota of conservative or neo-conservative doctrine to be visible in operations. But the largest single departure from traditional principles was one in an area equally or more cherished on the liberal side of US politics: respect for law. Legalism has been fully as much a tradition in American foreign policy as moralism: possibly more so. Perhaps any federal government, aspiring to be a government of laws, has normally a tendency to embody itself in the actual world as a government of lawyers, and therefore legalism is one of the elements expected in most policy-attitudes in such governments. But it appeared conspicuously at a discount in the Reagan years. The assorted attacks on Libyan targets (the 1981 shooting down of two aircraft and the 1986 punitive strikes) could be pragmatically defended as sending strong signals to a regime that had provoked them, or morally defended as due retribution for a proclaimed support of terrorism, but it was difficult to see how they could be squared with the normal legal conventions of sovereignty. The admitted US disinformation campaign against Libya, dreamed up by Admiral Poindexter, has been presented as justified in terms of Churchill's famous phrase about truth needing the protection of a 'bodyguard of lies'. But that was said of wartime, and ever since Grotius's day the Western tradition of international law has held that there is a large distinction between what is legitimate in war and what is legitimate in peace.

On several other matters, even before the Iran imbroglio, the Reagan attitudes were again less legal-minded than the American norm. The mining of Nicaraguan harbours, for instance: similar action had been taken in Haiphong, it is true, but that was after several years of overt combat operations against the North Vietnamese government. Refusal of the compulsory jurisdiction of the World Court or its judgement on Nicaragua, along with refusal to accept the Law of the Sea convention were other instances. The Administration in general evinced a greater scepticism than its predecessors concerning international law as an instrument which could be relied on to accord a fair deal to American interests, the assumption basically becoming that the World Court was a 'packed' court which would always judge in accord with Third World pressures.

On the related question of faith in international organization, American official attitudes in the mid-1980s appeared almost as unfavourable as they had been in 1919, after the First World War, when the US refused membership of the League of Nations. The US quitted UNESCO, temporarily quitted the ILO and reduced its (exorbitant) contribution to the UN budget. Many spokesmen of the far right for a time proclaimed that they had so little expectation of useful action from the UN that they would contemplate its departure from American territory with no regret at all, and might even advocate the US quitting membership if further provoked by some particularly outrageous resolution passed by the Third World majority. In the Security Council, where the casting of an American veto had once been approached only with remorse and soul-searching, it became a routine mechanism of defence of American interests against a 'mechanical majority' on the other side. (As one US diplomat said, 'It's like adultery – at first you feel guilty but later it gets to be kind of fun.')

The temporary but vigorous display of decline in US esteem for, or even tolerance of, the UN could be seen as a specifically neo-conservative victory in that particular strand of foreign policy. Israel had tended to feel victimized by the UN ever since the mid-1950s, when the Arab delegations first began to exert effective lobbying techniques *vis-à-vis* delegations from other Third World countries, with results that in normal circumstances will always produce an anti-Israeli majority. One might even argue that possibly the clearest point on which the Reagan Administration departed from the precedents set by most postwar US administrations was its distinctly cavalier attitude to international organizations and international law. In the Iran imbroglio, of course, domestic law also was treated with some disrespect.

From a technical point of view, the most interesting thing about the Reagan period in American foreign policy may remain the dichotomy I have suggested between its operational and its declaratory signals. It is true that there is always some such gap for any administration or any government, but the contrasts seemed somehow more notable with President Reagan than with most other decision-makers. Possibly that was a sort of boomerang effect from his greatest political asset, his skill as a communicator. Precisely because he communicated assorted personal or ideological visions with such sincerity and conviction, the contrast between what was initially expected and how it all finally turned out became particularly vivid.

What was actually done – the substance of operational policies – really (as was noted earlier) showed a great continuity with the policies of the past. The alliances with Western Europe and Japan, essential to the stability of the central balance of power, were more or less safeguarded as they had been by every US Administration since Truman's, though considerably shadowed by trade disputes at the end of the period. The rapprochement with China was maintained, as it had been ever since President Nixon's time. The American spheres of interest in the Mediterranean, the Middle

East and the Persian Gulf were verbally asserted with even more vehemence than in the past. (That was however undoubtedly the least effective sphere of operational policy: the peace process begun in the Kissinger and Carter periods was not advanced, the Arab quasi-alliances came under great strain, the Iran relationship deteriorated still further, especially at the time of the tragic shooting-down of the Iran airliner in July 1988. Even the Israeli relationship suffered visible damage.) The policies in Central America and the Caribbean seemed by the end of 1988 to have dwindled towards compromise, and eventual American acquiescence in a Central American outcome more likely to leave Nicaragua in the hands of the Sandinistas than to help the survival of the Contras. In the rest of the Third World one can in general see (despite the 'Reagan Doctrine's' alleged achievements and stated ambitions) largely a continuation of the operational caution that had set in during Nixon's time. On South Africa, despite the initial criticisms of 'constructive engagement', the actual relationship between Washington and Pretoria worked eventually to produce useful movement on Namibia and Angola. In the field of arms and arms control, where the initial signals had seemed to imply a vast increase of military muscle and a positive allergy to arms control, the outcomes towards the end of the period, in fact, indicated general conformity to the existing postwar patterns; that is, expenditure on arms finished up at 5.9 per cent of GNP, compared to 5.5 per cent in 1981 when the decisions of the Carter period were still the major influence. So on average for the Reagan period as a whole, though arms-spending was certainly higher than in the post-Vietnam years, it was distinctly lower than the average over the previous three decades of the Cold War as a whole: about 6.1 per cent as against 8.6 per cent. Arms control negotiations, still more paradoxically, seemed to indicate greater promise than even during the heyday of détente in 1972.

On operational policies it was thus rather difficult to see in what areas any great differences between the Reagan years and those of his predecessors could be shown to lie. The major differences, therefore, have to be located in the sphere of declaratory policy; the major long-term intellectual debate on this eight-year patch of American foreign policy may be as to whether the Reagan declaratory policies were, on balance, useful or damaging in the achievement of American objectives.

At first glance, the answer must seem to be that they were on balance damaging. During the most notable disaster of the entire period, the Iran arms imbroglio, the visible dichotomy between operational and declaratory policy may be shown, as has been argued earlier, to have been the chief source of trouble. On Nicaraguan policy as well, one might argue that the fierceness of the initial declaratory signals probably helped convince the Sandinistas that they had no option other than to prepare for war to the knife, and that this assumption delayed a possible easing of tension such as eventually seemed to be emerging, whether for good or ill is a matter of political or ideological judgement. Throughout the period, in relations with America's major allies it was rather more often what was initially said than what was eventually done which evoked the fiercest criticism, especially from European liberal and left opinion. Indeed the critics' concentration on what was being said sometimes seemed to blind them to what was being done. For instance, one could hardly guess from European comment on the Reagan policies in Central America and the Caribbean (which evoked some of the most intense European polemics) that Washington during the Reagan years was waving as many carrots as sticks towards that area, in the funds promised for the Caribbean Basin Initiative and the proposals of the Kissinger Commission report. Even where strong-arm tactics were employed, as in Nicaragua, they were used with far less tough-mindedness than, for instance, Johnson had displayed in 1965 in the Dominican Republic or Eisenhower in 1954 in Guatemala, or even what Kennedy tried to do in 1961 in the Bay of Pigs fiasco in Cuba. But the initial declaratory signals had been so fierce that it was hardly surprising the commentators went on assuming that they conveyed the substance of policy, especially as such commentators usually had an ideological predilection for expecting the worst from right-wing Republican Presidents.

Despite all that, the final Reagan months could undoubtedly be presented, if given a little public relations gloss, as rather a period of halcyon weather in international politics, despite the Central American black spots. The Russians were continuing their process of exit from Afghanistan. The Angolans, Cubans and South Africans seemed to have settled on at least the outlines of a process by which the Cubans would depart from Angola and the South Africans cease their interventions there and even concede independence to Namibia. The Vietnamese were promising an early exit from Kampuchea. The process of destroying intermediate-range missiles in accordance with the treaty was visibly under way in both Western Europe and the Soviet Union. The American and Soviet 'top brass' were eagerly showing each other their more secret weapon systems. The Conventional Armed Forces in Europe talks seemed to offer NATO a prospect of equal ceilings in deployments of major forms of conventional military hardware like tanks and artillery, a prospect that could make possible the reduction or even elimination of battlefield and tactical nuclear weapons there. Negotiations on cutting the inordinate stockpiles of strategic nuclear missiles to half the existing warhead count were at least proceeding, even though there remained several obstacles. The largest war that had plagued the world during the Reagan period, that between Iran and Iraq, was ending on what had been the tacitly desired terms all along, from the point of view of the Western world, including the US: victory for *neither* side. And though it would be difficult to prove that Washington's policies had helped secure that outcome, on the whole the evidence seems to indicate that they at least marginally promoted it. The crucial question is: what factors induced the decision-makers in Teheran to accept a peace that, as Ayatollah Khomeini said, was more bitter than poison to him? And though the major factor was no doubt Iraqi success on the battlefield, at least a minor factor was the growing conviction in Teheran that the Americans would not let them win. In so far as American policy – by the naval patrol, the arms embargo and other measures – conveyed that signal steadily and forcefully to at least some of the policy-makers in Teheran, it must be accounted a success. But did the Administration consciously set out to do so? Or was it mostly luck?

The phrase I have used as the title of this chapter was spoken by Robert McFarlane when he was trying to enlighten the Congressmen enquiring into the Iran arms deal about what kind of support was given to the Contras during the period in which Congress had cut off funds. 'Basically', he said, 'it was all smoke and mirrors.' The fact that an image from the world of the stage magician – the specialist in the creation of dazzling temporary illusions – was what came to the mind of the former National Security Adviser while he was groping for understanding of the policies of the Administration in which he had himself served seems rather significant. Though McFarlane was only referring to Nicaragua policy, I would argue that there was a strong 'smoke-and-mirrors' element in a good many of the Reagan era policies. The President himself once said that communication was the heart of show-business. Did he also assume, perhaps unconsciously, that show-business was the heart of communication? If so, a conscious or unconscious technique based on that assumption must be said to have served him well enough personally. Not many Presidents have had so few or such mild dips in their popularity-ratings during eight years of office.

Looking back on the period as a whole, the making of American foreign policy often seems to have had, like some of the Hollywood epics of Ronald Reagan's earlier years, 'a cast of thousands', but no script-writer. That is, there seemed a great many people with 'bit parts' in the production but little evidence of a single mind in charge of a coherent design. That was hardly surprising considering the number of hands actually at work: two Secretaries of State, six National Security Advisers, two Secretaries of Defense with firm foreign policy views, along with Assistant Secretaries of State, lieutenant-colonels and retired generals in basements, special envoys and assorted ideologues, gurus and speech-writers *ad lib*. Plus, of course, in the final two years an entire chorus of Congressmen and Senators in full voice. Perhaps it will serve the textbooks as an example of dispersion of the decision-making process in a pluralist democracy.

Even more, it must surely stand as a case-study in the paradoxes of history and politics. A President who came to power vowing that the US would 'walk tall' again in fact oversaw policies that conduced to the rapid shrinking of American economic and diplomatic clout (and even autonomy) in the society of states. An Administration declaring its guiding star to be the light of sound conservative economic principles was to be described (by Professor Galbraith, for instance) towards the end of its patch of history as having practised 'irresponsible Keynesianism'. A mode of strategic analysis which in 1981 had seemed to prescribe a dedicated distrust of Soviet leaders, especially when they came bearing gifts in the arms-control line, eventuated by 1988 in a set of arms-control understandings and consequent strategic changes in Europe that seemed likely (for good or ill) to erode the diplomatic alignments of forty years. The great anti-terrorism drive boomeranged into the embarrassment of a disclosed effort to buy out hostages, even at the cost of providing arms to an obdurate and dangerous enemy. A political leader who had come to office amid a chorus of alarm among liberals about his alleged rigidity of stance and tendency towards 'confrontations' in the international sphere made his exit amid doubt on the right and applause on the left for the far-reaching nature of his arms-control agreements with the Soviet Union.

9. Bush and the Reagan Legacy

The world outside America watched the Presidential election of 1988 with equanimity shading into boredom. Once the more protectionist of the initial field of candidates for nomination had been eliminated, very little in the record of either of the two final contenders raised more than a slight *frisson* of alarm in most foreign opinion. That was quite a contrast to reactions, especially in Europe, to the 1980 campaign, when the Reagan rhetoric had created a notable level of anxiety well beyond the left.

On the other hand, if neither of the candidates in 1988 seemed alarming, neither inspired much optimistic expectation that his management of power would see a transformation of world politics, or even a dispelling of the sense of *déjà vu* that hung over Western diplomacy and strategy. If Dukakis had won, the parallel with Kennedy's advent after the eight Eisenhower years would no doubt have been drawn with wistful anticipation by Europeans still nostalgic for 'Camelot'. But, on the other hand, by 1988 that interpretation of the early 1960s looked a lot less convincing than it had done at the time, and the Eisenhower Presidency seemed more substantial than it had been then accounted.

More important still, during the final Reagan months when the campaign was reaching such molehill heights as it attained, the foreign policy establishments of the rest of the world, especially those in Europe, were focused chiefly on the far more dramatic sequence of changes in Moscow, as Mr Gorbachev consolidated his power, became President Gorbachev and pressed on with his attempts at remaking the Soviet Union. That drama very clearly held more possibilities of crisis than the staid constitutional process in the US.

Despite his many years of exposure to the media spotlights in Washington, George Bush, up to his election, seemed to retain beneath the bland and genteel surfaces of his personality an odd elusiveness as to his underlying qualities. The Democrats worked hard, of course, as the system required, to unearth dark secrets from his past, as far back as his time as a Navy pilot in the Second World War. The nearest approach to success in that endeavour came over the Iran–Contra affair, in which he might well have been judged to have been at least over-economical with the truth; likewise on the pre-crisis dealings of the CIA with General Noriega. But neither story seemed to have much impact on the campaign. Bush does not make a convincing villain, and though undoubtedly he was 'in the loop' of the decision-making process for most of the foreign policy choices of the Reagan administration, there seemed little evidence of his being an activist in many of them. Vice-Presidents usually have so restricted a constitutional role that only a high level of personal assertiveness gets them a large input into policy; Bush's reputation was not of that sort. Moreover, even if there had been evidence of a high policy-input on his part, it would probably have redounded to his advantage. American voters in 1988 were obviously by no means displeased or even doubtful about the effect of the eight Reagan years on America's standing in the world. Bush made that his most adroit and telling point in the first television debate with Dukakis when (questioned about 'Irancontragate') he asked that the whole record of the eight years, rather than one episode, be the basis for the people's judgement. Visibly a well-coached answer, and undoubtedly one to which most voters were responsive.

The contrast between the world of 1979, a very tension-ridden phase in international politics, and the prospective world of 1989 was clearly his best 'selling point' for what he was identified as offering: a continuation of the Reagan policies. In 1979 the Soviet–American confrontation, expressed as the Cold War, had been at its sharpest for decades: one might have said that there seemed hardly an inch of safety gained in the three decades since 1949. American relations with the Third World seemed far more abrasive than they had been then: no equivalent had been at that time imaginable for the American impotence and humiliation experienced in the confrontation with Ayatollah Khomeini. Even the gains made through the stable alliance with Western Europe seemed in doubt as NATO struggled with the 'two-tracks' policy on intermediate-range nuclear weapons. Ten years on, the relationship with Moscow had moved to a real, though unacknowledged, détente; US policies in the Third World, though still having their black spots (chiefly in Central America), also had some surprising successes. And the American alliance system had moved through the INF crisis to new quarrels, like a stormy multiple household regularly surviving its conflicts because, despite the rows, its continuance is seen as contributing to the security of all its members.

How much of the general improvement in the world scene during the Reagan years should be attributed to the policy choices of the Administration, as against luck, serendipity and external factors, like the advent of Gorbachev, has been a primary issue for the earlier chapters of this book. But it is hardly surprising that it was not an issue for the voters in 1988. George Bush, as Ronald Reagan's anointed political heir, undoubtedly had to base his own electoral fortunes on that legacy. A poll during the campaign found that even though most of those questioned thought Dukakis had won the first television debate, they also thought that Bush was more 'likeable' and more 'presidential', and that he would do better than Dukakis at maintaining US security (63 per cent to 24 per cent) and at dealing with President Gorbachev (56 per cent to 27 per cent).[41]

Only with regard to Central America and the Caribbean was there much expectation among analysts that Dukakis might prove the more adroit on a foreign policy issue. For that area, the expectation that he might be the more likely to break with the counterproductive policies of the past had an obvious basis in the two candidates' earlier statements. But even so, the history of US relations with Central America is so full of hopeful 'new starts' which came to nothing much that the people of the area would be entitled to argue that the differences between Democratic and Republican policy-makers had usually proved marginal. After all, it was a Democrat (Kennedy) who launched the Bay of Pigs invasion, and another (Johnson) who put troops into the Dominican Republic of 1965, a much larger operation than Grenada or Nicaragua.

The most valuable legacy of President Reagan to his successor was (in the view of almost everyone save the very far right) the remarkable mutation in superpower relations which set in during the final Reagan years. Of course, that may be judged rather more an outcome of Gorbachev's activism in summitry and arms control than of any initiatives decided on in the White House, but if

Reagan had been a different kind of person – more consistent, more suspicious – the Soviet gestures might have come to nothing much in Washington–Moscow relations, and might have caused considerably more trouble in the Western alliance. Whether one attributes that turn of history (which initially surprised most of the commentators) to an underrated level of American diplomatic success, or merely to a consistent level of Soviet economic failure, the mutation allowed a striking change in the agenda of world politics in the early 1990s, a period in which George Bush must be an important actor and might be the decisive one.

During the election campaign itself, the new harmonies being heard at the top level of international politics were not unambiguously an asset to the Vice-President in the contest for votes. His claim to speak as the voice of experience, and the crafty implication that Dukakis as a 'new hand' would be bound to get these delicate matters wrong, might have proved still more telling if the world had looked more tense and dangerous than it did in October–November 1988. The voters' inclination in a period of crisis is to 'rally round the flag'; that is, to increase support for the existing leadership. Probably 1956 offers the most striking example: the Suez crisis that year was brought to a head within a few days of the US elections, and though that infuriated President Eisenhower (who suspected his British, French and Israeli allies of choosing their moment deliberately) it certainly did not reduce his majority.

George Bush's majority, though less overwhelming, was quite substantial enough to leave little doubt as to his mandate. He carried forty states, and 54 per cent of the popular vote, though on a relatively low turnout: only a little more than half the electorate bothered to cast a vote.

As was noted in the introduction, the 1988 elections strengthened the pattern which has seemed to be emerging during the past few decades, of the Presidency as a fief of the Republicans and Congress as a fief of the Democrats. One might almost say that the voters seem to have decided intuitively that the system of checks and balances, integral to the Constitution, needs that reinforcement. No doubt the results will continue to be disconcerting at times to outsiders used to parliamentary structures in which it could not happen. But American experience, including that of the late Reagan years, indicates that the US system can work reasonably well, sometimes even to advantage, under this pattern of the distribution of power. Lingering memories of an alternative possible pattern, a Democratic Presidency and a Republican Senate as in the late Truman years, possibly account for the anxiety with which the division of authority is sometimes regarded outside America. It might impede the new President in domestic affairs, particularly regarding appointments, as in the case of John Tower, and Budget cuts, but in foreign policy matters the situation should strengthen Bush, as a moderate Republican, against any remaining far-right wild men in his own party who might, for instance, want to block some arms-control agreement with the Russians.

Since foreign and defence policy issues played no decisive part in the campaign, one could regard Bush as entering office with fewer really fixed commitments in those areas than most of his predecessors, including Reagan, who had, of course, campaigned very heavily for stronger defences and more tough-mindedness towards deceitful Russians and perfidious Third World governments. It is true that Bush had conveyed the general commitment to carry on with the good work of the Reagan period, but by 1988 that could as readily be interpreted to mean summitry and arms-control agreements as to mean the striking of pugnacious stances towards the outside world.

Earlier chapters have noted the extraordinarily pluralistic and diverse (even fragmented) style of foreign policy-making in the Reagan years as one explanation of some of its paradoxes. Two Secretaries of State, two Defense Secretaries, six National Security Advisers, a CIA chief, at least five or six of the Assistant Secretaries, one lieutenant-colonel of marines, and a substantial handful of White House personages (including the First Lady?) all left a visible fingerprint or two on American foreign policy in the Reagan years. Amid such a crowd it is admittedly rather difficult to discern any particular impact on the part of the Vice-President. But he did actually have rather better political standing than most Vice-Presidents in this arena, by virtue of the fact that early in the first term Reagan had decreed that he should take on the role of 'crisis-manager' for the Administration (much to the irritation of Alexander Haig, who felt the role belonged to the Secretary of State). Since, as was noted earlier, there were actually no true crises between Washington and either Moscow or Beijing during the Reagan years, one might tend to assume that the crisis-manager's role turned out to be no more than that of a shield-carrier standing in a corner of the set. But that is not the whole story, since crisis-avoidance is an even more valuable diplomatic technique than good crisis-management, and there may have been some conscious effort in that direction.

The period when it was most needed was undoubtedly 1981–3, from the peak of the Polish drama in late 1981 to the NATO exercises of late 1983. Mention was made earlier of the Soviet agent Oleg Gordievsky, who, as the head of the KGB station in London, had been 'turned' and was at the time reporting to MI6 on Moscow's anxieties. The British Secret Service would normally share such information with the CIA, and Bush, as an ex-Director of that organization and the official crisis-manager, would be the obvious person in the Washington political leadership to receive it. Gordievsky put the highest point of Soviet anxiety as November 1983: the US process of reassurance began with the Reagan speech of January 1984. That may have been a coincidence but it seems rather like the outcome of a decision that tension should be reduced a notch or two in the interests of crisis-avoidance.

A point was made in earlier chapters about the difference between the declaratory and the operational signals of the Reagan years: that is, between what the President said (which was initially often a hyped-up flight of moral and ideological rhetoric) as against what the Administration did, which was often sober and pragmatic enough. Since no one ever regarded George Bush as a notably articulate man or as one with the knack of turning a catchy political phrase (except 'voodoo economics'), it is unlikely that the wordsmiths who put together the bold declaratory signals (the President's speechwriters) ever asked him for ideas. His influence would therefore have tended to be confined to the operational side of policy, especially when the system seemed to be drifting towards crisis, since he was officially the crisis-manager. There were, of course, some moments of idiocy there, chiefly 'Irancontragate', of which he must have had at least partial knowledge and perhaps rather more actual understanding than Reagan. He was also reported to have taken an active role in the policy on Libya and Grenada and on the Persian Gulf. One could certainly identify him, therefore, with the more tough-minded pragmatism of the Administration, but not with its ideological flourishes. Brent

Scowcroft, who was to become his National Security Adviser, called him a 'Rockefeller Republican', which in foreign policy would indicate traditional power politics. (Nelson Rockefeller was Dr Kissinger's original patron in the Republican élite.) So one could perhaps regard his election as a victory (at least for the time being) of conservatism over neo-conservatism as the dominant philosophy in Republican foreign policy. And that outcome had its merits, since in the phase of international relations opening at his inauguration, temperate power-politics seemed likely to prove the name of the game. In particular, that assumption would be a factor reassuring to the most important US allies, and perhaps even to the Russians.

After 1986, Washington's relations with Moscow had moved with so much speed on arms control and other matters that by the end of the Reagan period the West European foreign-policy establishments were sending visible signals that they would be glad of a pause to reassess their NATO strategies. That was in marked contrast to earlier phases in East–West relations (for instance in Dulles's time) when the Europeans were mostly given to complaining of American foot-dragging. Thus, though it was by no means the most urgent problem on Washington's agenda in foreign policy, 'pre-emptive damage-limitation' *vis-à-vis* the American alliance structure, in parallel with continued engagement in the crucial processes of negotiation with the Soviet Union (even before Bush's inauguration, with the Gorbachev visit of December 1988) was one of the more useful ways for the new President to sharpen up his existing foreign-policy skills.

Though few of the decision-makers of America's allies had remained immune to President Reagan's well-attested personal charm, even fewer, if candour were a diplomatic habit, would have been given to praising his understanding of the strategic problems of the Western alliance or the economic problems of the late twentieth century. The general impression of the Reagan administration as intellectually a very ramshackle enterprise was much increased at the end of the period by the 'kiss and tell' memoirs of various of its ex-members, with their allegations of reliance on astrologers and the revelation that even Mr Reagan's 'spontaneous' words of wisdom on historic occasions may have been strictly inventions of his press officer. America's allies had reason to be grateful for the long economic boom of the last six

Reagan years which survived even the great Wall Street crash of 1987, and for some other aspects of 'Reaganomics' which, however, academically dubious, had considerably profited the fast-growing European and Japanese economies. There were also the hopeful arms agreements. But not many observers in the West had been inclined to attribute much coherence to the Reagan economic and foreign policies. The successes tended to be put down to his famous luck and the efforts of one or two aides, rather than good Presidential judgement. The *Economist*, which not infrequently reflects the assessments of the foreign-policy establishments of Western Europe and is enthusiastically in favour of the American alliance, was nevertheless prepared bluntly to describe Mr Reagan, in its issue of 10–16 September 1988, as 'the laziest and most ignorant' of the world's recent Western decision-makers. So in terms of personal Presidential input into understanding contemporary problems and devising modes of coping with them, almost any successor would have been regarded with a more hopeful eye.

Besides, Mr Bush was, in fact, not only personally well acquainted with most of the decision-makers of America's allies, he is the variety of American that the conservative foreign-policy élites in Europe find easiest to understand and deal with: East Coast establishment internationalist, upper class, Ivy League, an experienced insider in the spheres of diplomacy and intelligence work, and mildly 'hawkish'. So though they would not, on his record, be expecting a man of ideas, still less an intellectual giant, their assumptions must initially be far more sanguine than they had been with President Reagan. The only asset that could be seen as lost with the succession of Bush would be perhaps some communication skills, and that particular kind of talent is not one that comes at the top of their list of priorities. Moreover, the aides and policy-makers whom Bush was reported likely to appoint in international politics and international economics appeared much more in the mainstream of moderate conservative Atlanticist opinion than the 'California mafia' or the neo-conservative 'wild men' whose influence they had feared in the early Reagan years.

So even if one took the dismissive view that Bush was likely to prove just 'Reagan-and-water', as did many European analysts initially, that prescription was by no means seen as unpalatable by the relevant foreign policy élites. A continuation of Reagan policies, somewhat further attenuated by pragmatism and preferably less striking in their declaratory formulations, could suit many of the decision-makers of America's allies very well. In an international system which had become by 1989 astonishingly fluid in several areas, any signals of radical new thinking in the White House might have evoked more anxiety than cordiality, since they would be seen as threatening an overload of uncertainties in a world balance already seen as full of them.

In the later stages of the campaign, allied opinion, like domestic opinion in the US, moved predominantly in favour of Bush, especially after Dukakis, perhaps in a moment of desperation, raised the spectre of a sharpened American economic nationalism, apparently appealing to grass-roots resentment of foreign ownership and foreign investment in American industry and real estate. A move to curb the inflow of foreign funds into the US might well upset the delicately balanced applecart on which the prolonged boom of the Western economies was riding. That was one of the central issues of the election for the world outside America, and on it, as on the other vital issues – East–West relations, arms control, the necessities of adjusting cautiously to the enormous changes in the communist world, controlling the growing risks in the Middle East, burden-sharing in NATO – George Bush had by the end of the campaign come to seem a much safer bet than Michael Dukakis. Only on the Central America issues did there still seem to remain a consensus that Dukakis's attitude held more promise of reform.

All that being said, it remained the case that President Bush faced quite a few complexities with the decision-makers of America's major allies. The Reagan years had produced side-effects which would have complicated future decision-making for any successor, particularly in economic dealings with Europe and Japan. By the time of the 1988 election campaign, the US national preoccupation with the budget deficit and the trade deficit had further widened the tendency, in the political arguments, to look for foreign scapegoats. As many Americans saw it, the failure of some powers to carry their fair shares of the financial burden of collective defence was the most obvious focus of irritation. It could not escape the oratory of political candidates that the figures for the budget deficit and the trade deficit during the late Reagan years had both hovered not far from the $150 billion mark, which happened to be the figure usually postulated as the US contribution to the defence of Europe. That figure is quite misleading when taken to indicate what would be saved by redeploying the troops back home. Nevertheless, there was the valid and undeniable point that the US during the Reagan years had spent on average about 6.1 per cent of its GNP on defence (dropping in the final year to 5.9 per cent), whereas its most successful economic competitors, Japan and West Germany, had spent only about 1 per cent and 3.1 per cent respectively. Moreover, the dollar had fallen dramatically against both the yen and the mark, the US national debt had shown a sudden mountainous growth, and foreigners, especially the British, the Dutch and the Japanese, had been eagerly buying up American assets. In the words of the *Economist* (30 April 1988): 'By making it necessary for the dollar to fall so far, President Reagan's economic policy in effect put the US economy up for sale.'

All that operated to create the hangover of resentful American economic nationalism which had been expressed most clearly in some Dukakis speeches, along with the protectionist pressures in Congress and demands for more equal burden-sharing in collective defence on the part of major allies. Some change in that latter economic relationship has been overdue and would have been inevitable whichever candidate had succeeded. The convention by which Japan and most members of NATO (other than Britain) spend far less of their respective GNPs on defence than the US is a hangover from the earliest days of the Cold War, when the United States was vastly more prosperous than any of the others and their economic and political recovery was among Washington's primary concerns. But that had long ceased to be the case. Assuming the Administration sets itself an objective of reducing US defence costs towards 5 per cent of GNP (as would be very beneficial to the budget deficit), it would only be logical that the major and prosperous European members of NATO should also be expected to allocate about 5 per cent of their respective GNPs to defence. That would not imply any great change for Britain, whose defence costs have hovered round that level for the past 15 years and sometimes been above it, as in the early 1980s. France also has remained relatively close to that figure, but not so Germany or Italy, still less Japan.

Perhaps some of Mr Reagan's famous luck had lingered for Mr

Bush on this issue, however. As he took office, there was almost an *embarras de richesses* on the 'top table' of the world's arms control negotiators, several of the proposals showing real promise of feasibility even if he is only given one term (The contrast with the situation at the beginning of Reagan's first term was truly striking.) The proposal to which Bush most committed himself as candidate was the convention on chemical and bacteriological weapons: the chief remaining obstacles were in the field of verification. The START negotiations, looking for reduction of long-range strategic nuclear missiles to about half their existing levels, seemed also close to a possible treaty, the most substantial remaining obstacles being the arguments over sea-launched cruise missiles and the SDI. The most astute and experienced of America's arms-control negotiators, Paul Nitze, had floated the notion of a ban on ship-launched tactical cruise missiles, a move which would have quite real strategic advantages for the US and perhaps help to promote the conclusion of the START agreement. That in turn could see some actual reduction of nuclear stockpiles, incidentally allowing closure of some very dangerous weapons facilities in the US, thus providing an environmental bonus, along with substantial economies.

However, from the standpoint of Mr Gorbachev and the Europeans, as well as that of both sides' budget deficits and cost-cutting hopes, the top priority would logically be the Conventional Armed Forces in Europe talks which opened in early March 1989. Conventional armaments account for a much higher proportion of total defence expenditures than do nuclear weapons: at least 80 per cent on average of the relevant budgets. The conventional stability talks are based on the premise that 'common ceilings' should be established in the European theatre for major weapons-systems like tanks and artillery. Since Soviet forces deploy very much larger numbers of such weapons than NATO forces that would, of course, mean 'asymmetric cuts', much larger on the Soviet than on the Western side. For instance, a ceiling for tanks of 20 000 on each side would see the Soviet level cut very drastically (from 52 000) and the Western level cut only quite moderately (from 22 000). Similarly, on major artillery pieces the present Soviet level of 36 000 and the NATO level of 10 600 would both, possibly, come down, to about 10 000.

Such a concession may seem unlikely, but it was Mr Gorbachev's own principle:

> If there is any imbalance, we must restore the balance, not by letting the one short of some elements build them up, but by having the one with more of them scale them down.[42]

Moreover, concessions of this sort would have several advantages even from the Soviet point of view. The whole case for NATO's tactical and battlefield nuclear weapons in Europe is based on the proposition that they offer the only mode of offsetting Soviet superiority in numbers of conventional weapon systems. Once possible parity in conventional systems comes into even distant prospect, therefore, the rationale of NATO's battlefield nuclear weapons is undermined. In consequence, the existing NATO proposal for the modernization of such weapons would become very much less likely to go through. It is already under considerable attack in West Germany: naturally enough, since nuclear weapons of this range (under 500 kilometres) must almost inevitably land on German soil, either east or west. However, modernization has been strongly pushed by the NATO high command which looks to the prospective updated weapons to compensate for some of the gaps in their 'escalation ladder' left by the removal of intermediate-range missiles by the INF Treaty. Modernization was also supported by the US, Britain and France and some other NATO powers, so arguments on the issue had considerable capacity to drive a wedge into the heart of the alliance. And from the point of view of the Soviet high command, retirements of old weapons could be so arranged as to permit a modernization of Soviet systems and possibly also be traded against a reduction of the forward-based dual-capable strike aircraft, in which the West has an edge. So there was something for almost everyone in the potential 'package' which could be envisaged (including large budget cuts) though, of course, it will be long and vigorously argued on all sides before being actually put together.

Success in the conventional arms control field (and preferably the others as well, obviously) would make it much easier to freeze the US defence budget at its 1988 level (about $300 billion), which would in turn result in its dwindling as a proportion of GNP and so help reduce the overall budget deficit. Since George Bush categorically opposed increased taxes during the campaign, he must rely primarily on cutting costs to bring the deficit under control, at least in his present term, and defence spending certainly appears the area with most fat to cut.[43] According to Professor Martin Feldstein, who had been among the previous Administration's most influential economic advisers, a budget freeze, even without any new taxes, might reduce the budget deficit towards about 1 per cent of GNP during the early 1990s.

Conventional denunciations of the budget deficit and the trade deficit from both outside and inside the US had tended to obscure the fact that, despite their real though somewhat exaggerated disadvantages, they also had real uses, both domestically and globally. Rapid and complete elimination of either was obviously not at all likely, and if it were tried it might incur more risks than it averted. The budget deficit, running at about 3 per cent of GNP in the late Reagan years, had to be regarded, on its results, as a textbook demonstration of unavowed Keynsianism helping create and sustain the long boom of 1982–8. It could not be rapidly eliminated without adding to the factors which might tend to precipitate a sharp world recession in the early 1990s.

Similarly, without the US trade deficit some rapidly developing economies in the Third World, which were heavily dependent on sales to the American market, would not have enjoyed their notable level of prosperity. The reduction of the trade deficit had likewise to be a gradual process, dependent on a continued increase in American price-competitiveness, with possibly a further fall in the value of the dollar by as much as 25 per cent. Assorted other international adjustments might also be required, such as higher domestic consumption in Japan, a role for the yen as a reserve currency, expansion of the West German economy, and possible revaluation of the currencies of Taiwan, South Korea and Hong Kong, all of which, like Japan, were running very large surpluses on current account. So complex a set of adjustments in the structure of world trade must necessarily be a slow and strongly resisted process. It was, however, one that the new Secretary of State James Baker would find within his sphere of expertise from his time at the Treasury. Baker also had experience of the other intricate financial problem hanging over the world economy, that of Third World debt. On the whole, its dangers had been kept under rather better control during the Reagan years than had been predicted, by techniques sometimes referred to as 'market-oriented muddling-through', but a further cautious bid to resolve the problem was clearly indicated in the Bush years, especially as Baker had already in 1985 proposed a plan to that end. Fear of open default by a large debtor such as Mexico, which might shake the credit-structure of the American banking system, had been a persistent spectre in Washington. (It appeared to have raised its head again towards the end of the election campaign, when Mexico suddenly received an unsolicited offer of a large US loan, presumably because someone in Washington was worried about what such an event, in the final days, might do to Mr Bush's chances of election.)

To revert to the problems of America's alliance relationships: while a freeze on US defence spending might mean that the NATO allies and Japan would have to carry rather more of the burden of common security, it would not necessarily be altogether undesirable from their points of view. For one thing, the US projects most likely to be cut back or delayed would include those with most potential for encouraging unilateralism on the part of some future US Administration: SDI, and the very large naval forces which in the Reagan years were rationalized by a concept which some allies found alarming, the maritime strategic doctrine. For another thing, nationalism has tended to grow vigorously with economic success in both Western Europe and Japan. The sense of excessive strategic dependence on Washington, once accepted as inevitable, had therefore come to seem rather irksome. A more equal 'European pillar' in NATO and a more equal European voice in major decisions were hankered after among the European members of NATO, even in political quarters where they had previously hardly been audible, such as West Germany. (The arguments over the modernization of the battlefield nuclear weapons will much increase that tendency.) Obviously, it will be easier for the 'European pillar' to reach equality if its American counterpart is somewhat reduced in height. Diminished American ascendancy in NATO could also encourage the reintegration of France into the coalition. That is a process already under way in a slow and tentative manner, mostly via French co-operation on various strategic projects with West Germany and with Britain. A 'quadripartite' directorate of NATO (US, Britain, France and West Germany) would not be implausible as a concept for the 1990s. (That would provide France with redress for the snub de Gaulle got from Eisenhower in 1958, when he suggested a 'tripartite' directorate for NATO. Eisenhower's casual brush-off on that occasion was the distant origin of France's pull-out from the coalition a few years later.)

Assuming that the economic integration of Europe proceeds on schedule by 1992, the Europeans will then need a new objective in their gradual evolution of a durable partnership. The creation of a defence community to match the economic community would seem to offer a reasonable next objective. And the military cohesion of Europe as a separate entity in world affairs would be a logical development in what seems to be emerging as a changed phase in the central balance of power, in which it is becoming multilateral rather than bilateral.

In fact, the enormous economic success of Western Europe which almost certainly can only be greater after 1992, when seen alongside the relative economic failure of Eastern Europe and the Soviet Union, has begun to make that part of the world hauntingly resemble its late nineteenth-century incarnation, when Western Europe was very much the dominant partner. However economically desirable and perhaps inevitable, the process of change in such a direction would be pregnant with potential crisis. If Eastern Europe becomes even more restive within the bonds of Comecon and even more resentful of Soviet tutelage, the process of attempted 'breakaway' could generate sudden large dangers to the peace. On the other hand, it will be difficult for policy-makers in Washington to maintain either American or European interest in a system constructed to meet a sense of threat from the Soviet Union during a time in which that sense of threat has largely vanished.

That is what I had in mind in the observation that President Bush would face a set of international issues more hopeful but also more complex than those facing his predecessors, either Republican or Democrat, in the past few decades. Policy-making from 1949 to 1989 was wonderfully simplified by the assumption of a determinedly hostile and potentially expansionist Soviet Union, whose troops were in firm control of a clearly defined line in Central Europe. Contingency plans could be made on the standard concept of a Soviet drive westward from bases in Eastern Europe, along the known feasible invasion routes. Targets could be assigned and troops maintained and exercised to meet such well-defined contingencies. But the continuation of Soviet control in Eastern Europe no longer, by 1989, looked as permanent as once it did. It had become possible for the German Chancellor to raise again in Moscow the notion of German reunification, an idea that had been tacitly almost abandoned since 1955. British and American spokesmen could even mention the possibility of pulling down the Berlin Wall, though the idea had of course a very frosty reception among the party bureaucracy in East Germany. If Eastern Europe, including East Germany, did not have to be seen as permanently in the Soviet sphere, that would transform the whole balance of power in the world and certainly greatly increase the diplomatic clout of Western Europe. It might also conduce to a new and dangerous wave of East–West confrontations as well as the revival of old feuds.

However, those historical processes may not fully crystallize in the earliest Bush years, perhaps not even during the first term. The most immediate crises requiring Washington's attention are likely to be more recently familiar ones, chiefly in Central America and the Middle East.

One event in the early Bush months which the President himself had attempted to defuse by a visit to Beijing after the Hirohito funeral was the long-awaited summit meeting between the chief decision-makers for China and the Soviet Union. The political demonstrations in China at the time of the Gorbachev visit of May 1989, and the subsequent massacre at Tienanmen Square of course rendered all previous calculations null and void, and ensured that the first crisis of the new Administration would be over human rights and embassy sanctuary in China. In the longer term, Soviet policy makers may face equal complexities. The three conditions that China originally imposed for better relations appeared to be at least in prospect of fulfilment at the time of Bush's election: Soviet exit from Afghanistan, a Soviet pull-back of its forces from the Chinese border and the exit of Vietnamese troops from Kampuchea. But those three issues may prove just the jagged peaks above the water of a great iceberg of potential Soviet–Chinese differences. The ideological component in that great iceberg of differences may be melting in the current of political turmoil in both countries, but the territorial component can hardly do so. It may, of course, stay unimportant for the rest of this century, or at least for the Bush period, even if he gets two terms. But the Chinese are a people with very long historical memories. When China is truly a great power again it will be able to afford to remember how much of the old Chinese Empire was lost only in the late nineteenth century to the old Czarist empire. The Russians have been nervous, ever since Stalin's time, that a reckoning might some day be presented for those acquisitions and they are not likely to grow more relaxed about the matter as China maintains its remarkable economic and military improvement in strength. So the long-term relationship between China and the Soviet Union is basically more ambiguous than that between China and the West.

There will have to be decisions very early in the new term on what, if anything, to do about Central America. Bush does not seem to have the same level of ideological commitment as Reagan to the anti-communist crusade in the area, despite his involvement with supplies to the Contras. And perhaps 'Irancontragate' has operated as a warning against heavy new involvement. The Contra organization appeared to have withered on the vine during the American electoral campaign months when it was getting no funds or attention. The numbers of guerrillas were reported in late 1988 as down to a few thousand, huddled in camps along the borders without ammunition or supplies. So they will perhaps mostly be transmuted from a military problem to a refugee problem, and join the Cubans in Miami.

On the other hand, United States' attitudes to Hispanic neighbours in general may well have been hardened by the 1988 electoral debate, because of the promotion of the drugs traffic to the status of a foreign policy issue. The proposition that young Americans were more immediately endangered by drug-runners than by the communist threat was impossible to deny in 1988, but it could be held to carry the unfortunate implication that the governments, or even the peoples, of Bolivia, Columbia, Mexico, Panama and the Central American and Caribbean area were engaged in a profitable form of aggression against US citizens. So despite the emergence and apparent survival of the Arias peace plan and the dwindling of the Contras, the omens for US policy in that part of the world did not seem good. (Relations with Thailand and Turkey might also be somewhat damaged by the concept of the drug-traffic as a form of war, but the primary source of concern seemed to be the Latin American-based trade in cocaine and crack.)

One could more hopefully argue that by the end of the Reagan years Central America had become less likely to generate a direct true superpower crisis than had been the case when he came to power. That was chiefly because both superpowers had indicated the limits of their willingness to confront each other in the area. The Soviet Union had never been at all likely to risk a 'Cuba 1962' kind of confrontation over arms supplies to Nicaragua, but in the early Reagan years the President (and some of his more hawkish aides) had been widely believed (especially outside America) to be willing to risk the combat involvement of American troops to bring down the Sandinistas. By the end of 1988 that appeared to be no longer the case, if it ever had been, and the amount of trouble the Administration had incurred over the effort to keep supplies going to the Contras in defiance of Congress seemed likely to discourage his successor from going down the same path, unless and until some further radical deterioration (from a Washington point of view) occurred in the area.

It had even begun to seem possible, by the beginning of the Bush years, that Cuba would cease to be so much a thorn in the American flesh as it had been for the previous three decades, ever since Castro's consolidation of power in 1959. That was not because of any sign of Cuba's move in the direction of *perestroika*, but rather because of Castro's apparent sense that the Russians in Gorbachev's time were distancing themselves from Cuba, especially after the demotion of Ligachev. Castro was reported to have said to a group of astonished diplomats in Havana: 'If the changes go on in the USSR, they will soon be describing us as those madmen in the Albania of the Caribbean.' Soviet publications were allegedly being censored in Cuba because of the effect that accounts of *glasnost* and *perestroika* might have on the attitudes of Cubans to their own economic problems which had grown more acute with the cuts in Soviet aid. If Gorbachev ever decided that Cuba was an expensive luxury which had to be sacrificed in the interests of more Western financial aid for the Soviet Union and better relations with Washington, Castro would be vulnerable indeed. But there would be great political obstacles within the Soviet Union to any such decision.

Even likelier than Central America and the Caribbean to see an early crisis needing American attention was the Middle East. The Israeli elections, just a few days before those in the US, produced a government which seemed certainly no more inclined than its predecessor to make any concessions to Palestinian national feeling, as expressed in the *intifada*. Moreover, with the Iran–Iraq war moving, though in a slow and halting fashion, from a cease-fire towards truce or armistice and in time a peace settlement, the Arab states would be able to turn their attention from the Gulf back to their normal preoccupation with Israel. Some of them had acquired more advanced armaments, especially long-range missiles from China and elsewhere, which could carry chemical as well as high-explosive warheads. The Israeli temptation to pre-empt by air-strike, as in the case of the Iraqi nuclear reactor, would be very high during a crisis, and that could involve, for instance, Saudi Arabia as well as Iraq in any future conflict.

During the campaign Bush took a slightly less pro-Israeli stance than Dukakis on, for instance, the highly symbolic issue of moving the US Embassy to Jerusalem, which would be much resented by the Arabs. Despite the neo-conservatives, the Jewish vote was predominantly (about 75 per cent) with the Democrats and Bush was less strongly identified with Zionist sympathies than Reagan had been, so the chance of a new American initiative finding some favour with the Arabs was perhaps better than during the Reagan years. The beginnings of change were symbolized, however, by the Reagan policy-makers' decision, before they made their exit, to begin conversations with the PLO in Tunisia. The Palestinians had shown a different kind of military capacity with the *intifada*, and by then a new political self-definition with the declaration of a Palestinian state, and prospectively a provisional government. Yasser Arafat and King Hussein had also changed their stances in ways that seemed to allow for the emergence of a Palestine–Jordan confederation. New roles for both the United States and the Soviet Union seemed possibly foreshadowed in the next effort at a settlement.

The world balance of power changed a great deal in the Reagan years; ironically, largely in directions contrary to those eagerly expected by his most fervent supporters when he entered office. The optimism of the early days, with the slogans about 'walking tall' and 'morning again in America' had given way temporarily in the final Reagan year to a widespread American intellectual anxiety that the United States was well advanced along the path that earlier great powers and empires (such as Britain) had followed: military over-spending with consequent neglect of the level of domestic investment necessary for increased productivity and so an eventual need to abdicate from over-ambitious commitments. It was not difficult to read signs of that historical syndrome into the Reagan years, but equally one was obliged in the same period to see still more striking symptoms of the equivalent condition, or worse, in the Soviet case. So what really appeared to be coming into view by the Bush inauguration was a still more important development, likely to shape the future for Bush and his successors well into the new century.

One might call it a sort of dwindling of both superpowers' ascendancy over the rest of the society of states with, in consequence, an easing of the tensions between them. That is to say, the society of states appeared to have moved during the eight Reagan years a visibly large notch further along the way from the original bilateral balance of power of the immediate postwar decades (dominated by the central 'adversary pair', the United States and the Soviet Union) towards the emerging multilateral balance, long foreseen. That tended to foster a far more dispersed and complex pattern of power-centres and power-rivalries in the society of states. One consequence would in logic be a reduction in tension between Washington and Moscow. The arms-control agreements and assiduous 'summitry' of the final Reagan years seemed a first symptom of this change.

The law of unintended consequences operated very powerfully in the Reagan period; so that an administration which came to office vowing a reassertion of American values and power in the society of states in fact chose policies which tended over the long term to diminish American influence on world affairs. The way it happened, and the reasons why, will no doubt be future issues for debate. But in Bush's early months of office it seemed probable that the changes in the relationships between the dominant powers would on balance prove fortunate rather than the reverse, allowing a continuance, in the final decade of the century, of the surprising détente of the late Reagan years, even though in the meantime they added to the diplomatic complexities in the pathway of President Bush.

The policy-makers round Bush, dealing with these complexities, had come to their tasks with a good deal more experience than was the case for the average 'newcomers' arriving with a just-installed President. If they fall short of what is required of them in the newly-fluid phase of international politics, opening with the final decade of the century, it will not be for want of knowledge, or lack of a sophisticated understanding of how the society of states works. It might be a shortage of what Bush was given to calling 'this vision thing'. During his first few months, the reproaches that came his way concerned his alleged excess of caution, and failure to make an imaginative mark on the astonishing new phase of world politics which seemed to have been offered by Mr Gorbachev and the turbulence of the communist world.

Notes

1. *New York Times*, 12 July 1985. Those interviewed were Irving Kristol, Norman Podhoretz and Midge Decter for the neo-conservatives, Richard A. Viguerie of the *Conservative Digest*, Burton Hale Pines of the Heritage Foundation, and Michael Novak of the American Enterprize Institute. Mr Novak perceptively remarked that Ronald Reagan had been from the earliest days in California, always 'a classic consensus politician', not an ideologue. Some of the other principal names associated with right-wing doctrine, policy-making or journalism such as George Will, William Safire, Jeane Kirkpatrick, Richard Perle and Richard Pipes, among others, will be quoted in due course.
2. Paul Nitze, 'Atoms, Strategy and Policy', *Foreign Affairs*, 1956 vol. 54, no. 2 (January 1956).
3. Founded by Paul Nitze, who became the chief arms control strategist of the early Reagan years. Other members who attained political office included Jeane Kirkpatrick and Richard Pipes.
4. Norman Podhoretz, 'The Present Danger', *Commentary*, (March 1980).
5. This is a theory held by some Protestant fundamentalists that Armageddon – the final battle between good and evil before the end of the world and the millenium – is at hand. So the possible destruction of the world by nuclear war could be regarded as within the providence of God: a disturbing view to attribute to the chief decision-maker of the major nuclear power. But there was no evidence of President Reagan holding any such belief, or of his being much influenced in policy matters by any religious doctrine: he has been far less of a church-goer than Jimmy Carter.
6. In George Kennan, 'The Sources of Soviet Conduct', originally written as an awesomely long secret cable when

Kennan was a US diplomat in 1946 in Moscow, first published as an influential *Foreign Affairs* article by 'Mr X' while he was still a diplomat, republished with acknowledgement of authorship in 1952 in *American Diplomacy, 1900–1950*.

7. Irving Kristol, in *The Australian*, 26 January 1986.
8. Garry Wills, in Baltimore *Sun*, 22 June 1985.
9. Though there are some indications that Mr Gorbachev may be discarding it in favour of the alternative concept of the balance of power: an interesting change, if it persists.
10. See the author's *Negotiation from Strength: A Study in the Politics of Power* (New York: Knopf, 1963) for a more detailed account of the policy in its earlier incarnations.
11. Published in *Time*, 25 November 1985.
12. Ibid.
13. Stephen Meyer, 'Soviet Strategic Programmes and the SDI', *Survival*, vol. XXVII, no. 6 (November–December 1985) (Professor Meyer is at MIT. *Survival* is the journal of the International Institute for Strategic Studies.)
14. See 'The Maritime Doctrine', John Lehman and Admiral Thomas Watkins, US Naval Institute, January 1986.
15. *Wall Street Journal*, 3 June 1980.
16. *New York Times*, 30 January 1981.
17. Seweryn Bialer and Joan Afferica, 'Gorbachev's World', in *Foreign Affairs: America and the World 1985*, vol. 64, no. 3 (1986). See also Zbigniew Brzezinski, *Game Plan: How to Conduct the US–Soviet Contest* (New York: Atlantic Monthly Press, 1986).
18. Bialer and Afferica, 'Gorbachev's World'.
19. International Institute for Strategic Studies, *The Military Balance, 1986–87* (London: IISS, 1986).

The official counting of troops and hardware remained, as in earlier negotiations, an aspect of the diplomatic arguments. But a new candour did seem to be developing. By early 1989, IISS figures and official NATO figures, when appropriately interpreted, were not far apart.

	NATO	WP[1]	NATO	WP[1]
Divisions	105.3	101.3	103.0	224.3
Troops	2.34m	2.14m	2.21m	3.09m†
Tanks	22,000*	53,000	22,224*	51,500
Artillery	10,600	36,000	17,328‡	43,400‡
IFVs[2]	6,200§	23,600	4,728§	22,400
Combat aircraft	–	–	3,977	8,250
Attack aircraft	2,865	2,330	–	–
Fighters	1,178	4,432	–	–

[1] Warsaw Pact; [2] Infantry Fighting vehicles; † includes general support troops and air-defence troops excluded by IISS; * includes about 8,500 tanks in storage; ‡ includes large mortars, not included in IISS figures; § includes 575 Infantry Fighting Vehicles in storage.

20. *International Herald Tribune*, 19 June 1987.
21. *The Australian*, 20 July 1985.
22. *Time*, 28 April 1986.
23. *International Herald Tribune*, 23 April 1986.
24. He implied, for instance, that the Soviet decision-makers had found him less than truthful or reliable.
25. *New York Times*, 2 October 1982.
26. Editor of the *Middle East Policy Survey* writing in the *Guardian*, 4 May 1986.
27. Ibid.
28. Jeane Kirkpatrick, reprinted in *Dictatorships and Double Standards: Rationalism and Reason in Politics* (New York: Simon & Schuster, 1982).
29. Jeane Kirkpatrick, 'United States Security and Latin America', *Commentary*, January 1981.
30. See William R. Bode, 'The Reagan Doctrine', *Strategic Review*, vol. XIV, no. 1 (Winter 1986). Mr Bode was a Special Assistant to the Under-Secretary of State for Security Assistance, Science and Technology. For an alternative view, see 'The Guns of July' by Stephen S. Rosenfeld in *Foreign Affairs*, vol. 64, no. 4 (Spring 1986).
31. *Time*, 28 April 1986.
32. *A New Inter-American Policy for the Eighties: Report of the Committee of Santa Fé* (Washington: Council for Inter-American Security, 1980).
33. US Ambassador to Nicaragua, Lawrence Pezzullo, quoted in

Christopher Dickey, 'Central America: From Quagmire to Cauldron', *Foreign Affairs: America and the World 1983*, vol. 62, no. 3.

34. Excessively, because as a military operation it seems to have been rather clumsy given that the target was so small, the opposition forces so weak (about 650 Cuban troops from a construction corps) and the area so close to America's own shores that it should have been a 'walkover', and it was by no means that, as later reports established. Fourteen members of the Marxist faction which had seized power were in due course convicted of the murder of the Prime Minister and ten others.
35. See Chester A. Crocker, 'South Africa: Strategy for Change', *Foreign Affairs*, vol. 59, no. 2 (Winter 1980) for a fuller account.
36. Currently Finland has a rather conservative government, a vigorous free-market economy, and one of the highest standards of living in the world.
37. See for example David Watt, 'As a European Saw It', *Foreign Affairs: America and the World 1983* (New York: Council on Foreign Relations, 1984).
38. See *The Times*, 5 November 1987, and 6 November 1987.
39. Alexander Haig, *Caveat: Realism, Reagan and Foreign Policy* (London: Weidenfeld & Nicolson, 1984) p. 85.
40. David Stockman, *The Triumph of Politics* (New York: Harper & Row, 1986) p. 312.
41. The poll was published in *Time*, 10 October 1988.
42. For a more detailed account of the state of play of the major arms control negotiations at the end of the Reagan period, see the journal of the International Institute for Strategic Studies, *Survival*, September-October 1988. The Gorbachev quotation appears in an article by the former US Ambassador to the conventional arms control negotiations, Robert D. Blackwill, 'Specific Approaches to Conventional Arms Control in Europe', vol. XXX, no. 5.
43. For an account of the 'mismatch' between the extra defence costs of the Reagan years and any actual increase in military efficiency, see an article by a Defense Department official, Franklin D. Spinney, in the *International Herald Tribune*, 31 October 1988: 'Defense Program or Public Works Project?'.

Index

2140